THE FARMER AND THE HEN:

A LANCASHIRE LOVE STORY

The Poultry Industry in the Fylde 1845–1939

John Grimbaldeston

Published by Zaccmedia
www.zaccmedia.com
info@zaccmedia.com

Published January 2016

Copyright © 2016 John Grimbaldeston

The right of John Grimbaldeston to be identified as author of this work has been asserted by him in accordance with the Copyright, Designs and Patents Act 1988.

All rights reserved. No part of this publication may be reproduced, stored in a retrieval system, or transmitted in any form or by any means, electronic, mechanical, photocopying or otherwise, without the prior written permission of the publisher.

ISBN: 978-1-911211-00-6

British Library Cataloguing-in-Publication Data
A catalogue record for this book is available from the British Library.

The extract from *On Her Majesty's Secret Service* is reproduced with permission of Ian Fleming Publications Ltd, London, copyright © Ian Fleming Publications Ltd 1963.

Barney Smith, of the *Preston Digital Archive*, and Mike Hill of the *Lancashire Evening Post* kindly gave permission to reproduce four images: Preston Digital Archive: Poultry Market, Lune Street, Preston 1939. Lune Street and Wharf Street, Preston c. 1933; "Pubs of Preston." c. 1960, Landlord Dick Sumner inspecting the old cock loft in the New Cock Inn, Preston; and Poultry Market, Lune Street, 1939.

The extract from *English Journey* is reproduced with permission of United Agents on behalf of the Estate of the Late J B Priestley.

Front cover, upper picture:
Copyright © Shutterstock.com

Front cover, lower picture:
Preston Digital Archive: Lune Street Poultry Market c. 1933.

Cover design & typesetting by Zaccmedia.com

CONTENTS

Preface	v
Acknowledgements	vii
List of Illustrations	ix
Introduction	xvii
Chapter 1 The National Background	1
Chapter 2 The Mid-Lancashire Poultry Industry	39
Chapter 3 The Lancashire Utility Poultry Society	61
Chapter 4 Collinson's of Garstang	69
Chapter 5 Wrennall's of Barton	85
Chapter 6 Barron's of Catforth	95
Conclusion	109
Bibliography	115

PREFACE

Up until about 1850 the domestic fowl was the poor relation of the farming world, dismissed contemptuously as the "dunghill fowl," but by the 1920s hens were making a major contribution to the agricultural economy of the United Kingdom, and the central Lancashire area in particular was a major force in the poultry industry.

Fylde poultry dynasties such as Barrons, Collinsons, Wrennalls and Hamnetts entered and won prizes in international laying tests and exported their stock abroad. They were at the forefront of the development of poultry housing, equipment and feeds, and in improving strains of chickens, and yet the industry in the Fylde area has remained relatively undocumented. It is the aim of this book to begin to redress that omission, and to investigate why a relatively small area of the county should prove so successful in this branch of agriculture.

The book looks at the gradual national awakening to the economic opportunities provided by poultry, and then focuses on one particular area. A feature of the nascent poultry industry was the formation of clubs and societies where like-minded people met and exchanged ideas, and one of these societies, the Lancashire Utility Poultry Society (LUPS), is examined in some detail. Finally, the careers of three successful farmers are studied to see how and why they and their establishments prospered.

The main sources are the Lancashire Utility Poultry Society yearbooks, documents and business ephemera in the possession of the Fylde Country Life Museum and collected by the family of Jonathan Collinson, one of those successful farmers mentioned above, and newspapers and journals from the period, in particular the *Preston Guardian* and *The Feathered World*. Poultry "help" books from the late nineteenth and early twentieth centuries are also used. Chickens seem to attract an engaging breed of humans, and the comments and observations of numerous poultry fanciers have provided illumination. It is hoped that from all these sources a general picture of the mechanics behind a successful industry emerges.

ACKNOWLEDGEMENTS

Most of the material for this book has come through the Fylde Country Life Museum, a hidden gem of a museum at Farmer Parr's in Fleetwood, and in particular its curator, John Higginson.

Howard Walsh and the *Farmers Guardian* kindly let me sit in their offices and spend hours searching through their archives.

Barney Smith, of the brilliant Preston Digital Archive, and Mike Hill of the *Lancashire Evening Post* kindly gave permission to reproduce four images: **Preston Digital Archive: Poultry Market, Lune Street, Preston 1939.** Lune Street and Wharf Street, Preston c. 1933; "Pubs of Preston." c. 1960, Landlord Dick Sumner inspecting the old cock loft in the New Cock Inn, Preston; and Poultry Market, Lune Street, 1939.

The extract from *On Her Majesty's Secret Service* is reproduced with permission of Ian Fleming Publications Ltd, London, copyright © Ian Fleming Publications Ltd 1963.

The extract from *English Journey* is reproduced with permission of United Agents on behalf of the Estate of the Late J B Priestley.

ILLUSTRATIONS

1.1 The Earl's Pile, "winner of many battles"   2
Herbert Atkinson, *The Old English Game Fowl: Its History, Description, Management and Feeding* (London. The Fanciers' Gazette, 1891), p. 44.

1.2 From Preston Digital Archive's "Pubs of Preston." c. 1960, Landlord Dick Sumner inspecting the old cock loft in the New Cock Inn, Preston   3
Preston Digital Archive: https://www.flickr.com/photos/rpsmithbarney/11879529594/ 05/09/2015

1.3 White Dorkings   4
S. H. Lewer, *Wright's Book of Poultry: Revised and Edited in Accordance with the Latest Poultry Club Standards* (London. Cassell and Co., 1913), p. 333.

1.4 Queen Victoria's poultry house at Windsor   5
Illustrated London News, 23 December 1843, Issue 86, p. 408.

1.5 Royal birds: Cochins   6
S. H. Lewer, *Wright's Book of Poultry: Revised and Edited in Accordance with the Latest Poultry Club Standards* (London. Cassell and Co., 1913), p. 241.

1.6 Dark Brahmas   7
S. H. Lewer, *Wright's Book of Poultry: Revised and Edited in Accordance with the Latest Poultry Club Standards* (London. Cassell and Co., 1913), p. 263.

1.7 A rather severe-looking Richard Teebay   8
Sir Edward Brown, *British Poultry Husbandry: Its Evolution and History* (London: Chapman and Hall's, 1930), illustration facing p. 94.

1.8 Miss Cooper, 1st prize   10
John Baily, George Fisher and William Yarrel, "Prize Poultry, &C," *Illustrated London News*, 21 June 1845, p. 390.

1.9 The inside of an ideal hen house, c. 1869   14
Lewis Wright, *The Practical Poultry Keeper: A Complete and Standard Guide to the Management of Poultry* (London and New York. Cassell, Petter and Galpin, 1867), p. 216.

1.10 Mr Brindley's incubator   16
Lewis Wright, *The Practical Poultry Keeper: A Complete and Standard Guide to the Management of Poultry* (London and New York. Cassell, Petter and Galpin, 1867), p. 244.

1.11 The Hearson incubator   16
Edward Brown, *Poultry Keeping as an Industry for Farmers and Cottagers* (London. The Fanciers' Gazette, 1892), p. 68.

1.12 Mrs Cheshire's brooder   18
Lewis Wright, *The New Book of Poultry* (London. Cassell and Co., 1905), p. 100.

1.13 and 1.14 The old and the new way of raising chicks, 193   18-19
"Prosperous Poultry Farming in Lancashire," *Lancashire Daily Post*, 5 October 1931, p. 4.

1.15 The Egg Train   20
"Egg Train's Mission," *Western Gazette*, 9 July 1915, p. 11.

1.16 and 1.17 National Utility Poultry Society, 1930–1   22

Illustrations

NUPS medal in Fylde Country Life Museum, Farmer Parr's, Rossall Lane, Fleetwood FY7 8JP.

1.18 Devon trials, 1933 — 23
Western Times, 22 September 1933, p. 16.

1.19 An advertisement from a poultry manual — 27
W. Powell-Owen, *Poultry-Keeping on Money-Making Lines* (London. George Newnes, 1919), p. 257.

1.20 A fowl pest burial in Pilling in the 1960s — 31
From the Collection of John Higginson, Fylde Country Life Preservation Society.

2.1 Lancashire (excluding Furness), 1937 (pre-Local Government Act 1972) — 39
http://www.historic-images.co.uk/wp-content/uploads/2012/02/Map-of-Lancashire-from-1937.jpg 30/05/2015

2.2 Cock fighting as part of the Preston Guild celebrations — 40
"Preston Jubilee Guild Sept 2nd," *The Morning Chronicle*, 6 September 1802, p. 3.

2.3 Lancashire Agricultural Returns, 1884 — 43
"The Official Agricultural Returns," *Preston Guardian*, 1 November 1884, p. 4.

2.4 Thomas Sherdley's obituary — 45
Obituary of Thomas Sherdley, *Preston Guardian*, c. 1932. Cutting courtesy of the Sherdley family.

2.5 *Westmorland Gazette* article — 47
Undated article from the *Westmorland Gazette* among the Collinson papers in possession of John Higginson of the Fylde Country Life Preservation Society.

2.6 Sir Edward Brown and delegates at the 1934 conference   46
"National Poultry Council Officials in Preston," *Lancashire Daily Post*, 21 April 1934, p. 6.

2.7 Lancashire egg packers at work   50
Ministry of Agriculture and Fisheries, *Report on Egg Marketing in England and Wales* (London. HMSO, 1927), illustration facing p. 36.

2.8 Preston Digital Archive: Poultry Market, Lune Street, Preston 1939   51
http://www.historic-images.co.uk/wp-content/uploads/2012/02/Map-of-Lancashire-from-1937.jpg 30/05/2012

2.9 1933 LUPS testimonial to five stalwarts of the industry   53
From the papers of Jonathan Collinson held by John Higginson of the Fylde Country Life Preservation Society.

2.10 Cut-away Lancashire brooder cabin   54
Fylde Country Life Museum, Farmer Parr's, Rossall Lane, Fleetwood FY7 8JP.

2.11 Poultry Market, Lune Street, 1939 (Preston Digital Archive)   54
Preston Digital Archive and *Lancashire Evening Post* Archive: Preston 1800–1990 https://www.flickr.com/photos/rpsmithbarney/4298375187/ 15/09/2015

2.12 Day-old chicks being despatched to Romania from Blackpool Airport, 1936   55
From the Collection of John Higginson, Fylde Country Life Preservation Society.

2.13 Insulated box for transporting eggs for incubation   55
Fylde Museum of Country Life.

3.1 1934 presentation evening   65
Lancashire Daily Post, 15 November 1934, p. 4.

Illustrations

4.1 Delaware State Board of Agriculture Certificate, 1918   70
From the papers of Jonathan Collinson held by John Higginson of the Fylde Country Life Preservation Society.

4.2 The Collinson coal-fired brooder   72
From the Collection of John Higginson, Fylde Country Life Preservation Society.

4.3 The coal-fired brooder fully erected   72
"Poultry for Profit 1923." From the papers of Jonathan Collinson held by John Higginson of the Fylde Country Life Preservation Society.

4.4 The Collinson family business structure   73
"Poultry for Profit 1933," p. 3. From the papers of Jonathan Collinson held by John Higginson of the Fylde Country Life Preservation Society.

4.5 "Gloucester" incubators on the Collinson farm   74
From the papers of Jonathan Collinson held by John Higginson of the Fylde Country Life Preservation Society.

4.6 The Collinson stall at an agricultural show   76
Photograph from the Collection of John Higginson, Fylde Country Life Preservation Society

4.7 Lingart dry mash hopper   77
"Poultry for Profit 1920." From the papers of Jonathan Collinson held by John Higginson of the Fylde Country Life Preservation Society.

4.8 Collinsons' Mill, Church Street, Garstang, 1920s   77
From the Collection of John Higginson, Fylde Country Life Preservation Society.

4.9 Lancashire cabins on the Collinsons' farm – probably 1930s   78
From the Collection of John Higginson, Fylde Country Life Preservation Society.

5.1 Jack Wrennall, as drawn by "Furnival" of the *Lancashire Evening Post* — 85

5.2 The Wrennall trap nest — 88
From the papers of Jonathan Collinson held by John Higginson of the Fylde Country Life Preservation Society.

5.3 Wrennall night arks being loaded at the farm — 89
Photograph from the Collection of John Higginson, Fylde Country Life Preservation Society.

5.4 Wrennall portable cabins — 90
Photograph from the Collection of John Higginson, Fylde Country Life Preservation Society.

5.5 Diversification: Jack Wrennall advertisement — 91
Lancashire Daily Post, 17 February 1939, p. 11.

5.6 Pigs slaughtered on the farm on their way to the butcher — 91
Photograph from the Collection of John Higginson, Fylde Country Life Preservation Society.

5.7 The Wrennall "office," possibly posed as a joke … but possibly not! — 92
Photograph from the Collection of John Higginson, Fylde Country Life Preservation Society.

6.1 Tom Barron in 1913 — 95
Tom Barron, *How I Breed the 200 Egg Hen: A Complete Treatise of the Methods Used by Tom Barron, England, in Producing Heavy Layers* (Philadelphia. Tom Barron Publishing Co., 1914), p. 5.

6.2 Singleton Farm, 1908: Olive and Elsie Barron — 96
From the Collection of Gwen Marquis, former Barron employee.

Illustrations

6.3 An inevitable choice of name   98
Tom Barron, *How I Breed the 200 Egg Hen: A Complete Treatise of the Methods Used by Tom Barron, England, in Producing Heavy Layers* (Philadelphia. Tom Barron Publishing Co., 1914), frontispiece.

6.4 Success in South Africa   99
The Times, 25 August 1926, p. 13.

6.5 Roomy laying cabin   100
Tom Barron, *How I Breed the 200 Egg Hen: A Complete Treatise of the Methods Used by Tom Barron, England, in Producing Heavy Layers* (Philadelphia. Tom Barron Publishing Co., 1914), p. 31.

6.6 Hens in a run at the side of the cabin   101
Tom Barron, *How I Breed the 200 Egg Hen: A Complete Treatise of the Methods Used by Tom Barron, England, in Producing Heavy Layers* (Philadelphia. Tom Barron Publishing Co., 1914), p. 35.

6.7 Iowa advertisement   102
Wallace's Farmer and Iowa Homestead, 30 January 1938, pp. 18–74.

6.8 Tom Barron   105

6.9 Tom Barron's obituary in the *Manchester Guardian*   106
"In Brief," *Manchester Guardian*, 11 October 1955, p. 16.

INTRODUCTION

Franklin took a red pencil out of his breast pocket and leaned over the map. Glancing from time to time at the list, he made a series of red circles at seemingly unrelated points across Britain and Eire, but Bond noticed that they covered the areas where the forests of symbols were at their densest. As he made the circles he commented, "Aberdeen – Aberdeen Angus, Devon – Red Poll, Lancashire – poultry, Kent – fruit, Shannon – potatoes," until ten red circles stood out on the map. Finally he poised his pencil over East Anglia and made a big cross. He looked up, said "Turkeys" and threw his pencil down.[1]

So Bond, M. and Franklin, "The Man from Ag. and Fish," work out that Blofeld's master plan is to destroy Britain's economy by destroying Britain's agriculture. Poultry farming in Lancashire is in the top six – the other four remain unidentified.

Another English writer also noticed the preponderance of poultry in Lancashire as he journeyed by rail from Manchester to Blackpool:

The feature of this route, once you were outside the larger towns, seemed to me to be what we call in the North the "hen runs". There

The Farmer and the Hen: A Lancashire Love Story

were miles of them. *The whole of Lancashire appeared to be keeping poultry.*[2]

Statistics about the time that Priestley was writing show that 14% of all hens in England of holdings of one acre or more were in Lancashire.[3] But how did Lancashire's poultry industry achieve such prominence, and what circumstances combined to enable it to develop so successfully?

This book will look at the development of poultry farming in Great Britain as a whole, and then gradually adjust its focus to one area, and then one organisation of poultry producers within that area, and finally three specific case studies. The chronology will begin with the shadowy origins of poultry keeping, from birds kept for cock fighting by the "Fancy," through barn-door fowl kept for "hen money." The introduction of Asiatic and North American strains which improved size and laying capacity will be discussed, and then the gradual more scientific approach to breeding and the economics of production. It will end approximately with the onset of World War Two, though one or two of the sub-plots will be carried through to their conclusions beyond that date.

Notes

1   Ian Fleming, *On Her Majesty's Secret Service* (London. Penguin Classics, 2004), p. 201. Reproduced with permission of Ian Fleming Publications Ltd, London, copyright © Ian Fleming Publications Ltd 1963 www.ianfleming.com

2   J. B. Priestley, *English Journey* (London. William Heinemann, Jubilee edition, 1984), p. 216.

3   Ministry of Agriculture and Fisheries, *Agricultural Statistics lxvii* (1932), pt 1, Table 6, p. 73.

1
THE NATIONAL BACKGROUND

Cock Fighting

The dominant influence on the types of chickens bred in Britain before Victorian times was cock fighting.[1] There is evidence to suggest that certain qualities in game chickens, such as colour of plumage and length of leg, were important and so early attempts at breeding birds for specific qualities began, and by the nineteenth century distinct strains of game fowl had evolved.[2] Cock fights were not just local affairs, but county matches were arranged: Sir Walter Gilbey cites a letter from Sir Henry Saville to his cousin Plumpton inviting him to Sheffield to "see our good cocks fight, if it please you in the manner of our cocking. There will be Lancashire of one part and Derbyshire of another part and Hallamshire of the third part."[3] Herbert Atkinson describes Lancashire as one of the great counties for the sport,[4] and Lord Derby at Knowsley was a renowned breeder.[5] In noting the attributes of Old English Game – good meat, excellent layers, good mothers, hardy, needing little feed[6] – Atkinson is noting the very qualities looked for later by Lancashire's breeders of utility poultry.

Fig. 1.1 The Earl's Pile, "winner of many battles." Among the Fancy, a "pile" was a bird of mixed colours but with a proportion of white feathers.

By the reign of George I Gilbey regarded county matches as an institution, and Lancashire versus Cheshire was a frequent match.[7] In 1727 one of the largest ever matches was fought, between Preston and Wakefield. Twenty fights took place, one was drawn, Preston won 12 and a total prize money of 230 guineas. The wagering would have made the actual money involved much greater.[8]

Cock fighting imprinted itself on Preston's landscape by giving the name to several of its pubs: The Fighting Cocks, the New Cock Inn, The Old Cock.[9] Even up to the 1960s, evidence of a cock-fighting past remained.

The National Background

Fig. 1.2 From Preston Digital Archive's "Pubs of Preston." c. 1960, Landlord Dick Sumner inspecting the old cock loft in the New Cock Inn, Preston

Farmyard Chickens

In contrast to the care and attention lavished on the fighting birds, any birds about the farm were often an indeterminate mixture of breeds, referred to deprecatingly as "barn-door" or "dunghill" fowls, and used for meat rather than eggs. They were usually the responsibility of the women of the household.[10] It may have been that the traditional English hens and their game bird appearance were damned by this similarity because farmers deplored the effects of game bred for hunting on their farmland. George Beesley reported in 1849: "The effects of the depredations of the privileged beasts and birds on the crops of the farmers are too well known."[11]

Hunting and sporting men were antagonistic to poultry. Sir Edward Brown was clear that large farmers were afraid to take up raising poultry in case of conflict with the landowners: "It is not too much to say that preservation of foxes and game for shooting had done more to restrict progress in the Poultry Industry than any other influence."[12]

Early Breeds

Of the poultry which might be recognisable to later eyes, Dorkings were probably the most common as their meat was prized and the methods of fattening them closely guarded;[13] other original English breeds were the Sussex and then the Hamburgh, all of them prized mostly for their meat, but the latter two were increasingly prolific layers.[14] By the mid-nineteenth century Cochin and other Asiatic breeds were introduced into Britain; these were larger than the indigenous chickens, laid more eggs, and also laid brown eggs, which before the arrival of these hens had been completely unknown in Europe.[15]

Fig. 1.3 White Dorkings

The National Background

Cochin Mania

The poultry industry in Great Britain was given a huge boost by Queen Victoria who, in 1843, received five "Cochin" or "Shanghai" pullets and two cockerels of the same breed. The *Illustrated London News* of 23 December 1843 contained a description and drawing of the Queen's suitably palatial poultry house at Windsor.

Fig. 1.4 Queen Victoria's poultry house at Windsor. The birds at the forefront almost dwarf the Queen and Prince Albert in the rear.

The Queen employed a full-time poultry man, James Walter, and he began experimenting by crossing the new breeds with the traditional English Dorkings, with markedly improved results in the egg-laying capacity of the birds.[16] There is some doubt now as to whether these birds really were like the modern Cochins, or were actually Brahmas, but they were much larger than the chickens the general public were used to, and inspired what some called "Cochin mania."[17] Those in positions of influence tended to follow the Queen's lead, and poultry once again became a fashionable hobby of the aristocracy, just as cock fighting was made illegal.[18] Cochins attracted attention because of their "gigantic size, gentle disposition, profligacy, and the ease with which they could be kept in confinement," and a Dr Watts even suggested that children should learn "kind and gentle manners" from them.[19]

The *Illustrated London News* also showed an interest in a problem of keeping chickens for their eggs – cannibalism of eggs and other chickens – and how that problem had been cured. So along with an interest in chickens came an interest in breeding as a science and a fascination with the rearing of chickens as a problem-solving exercise, traits which continue to this day.

Cochins were further thrown into the public eye at the Birmingham Show in 1850. The "Cochin mania" gave the poultry industry an impetus nationally. They proved to be better layers than the majority of breeds then kept, particularly over the relatively fallow winter season, and so it was felt that possibly poultry could actually be economically viable

Fig. 1.5 Royal birds: Cochins

Fig. 1.6 Dark Brahmas

for both eggs and breeding stock.[20] However, breeders tended to admire them for their fluffy feathers as much as for their laying potential, and breeding for appearance rather than performance reduced poultry's economic importance; probably the most significant contribution of the Cochin was that it stimulated interest in other heavy breeds such as the Langshan, the Black Java, and most important of all, the Brahma.[21]

Exhibition Poultry

Cock fighting was banned in 1849, but the competitive element between poultry owners continued in other directions. Most local village shows had a poultry section, often promoted by the village innkeeper, and even this low-key exhibition system led to improvements in quality. By 1852 the *Cottage Gardener* was lauding exhibitions for extending the taste "for the purer and better breeds of poultry."[22] Poultry competitions were small, and the method by which the winner was selected was an engagingly simple process of elimination. Two birds were put upon a table, their merits or otherwise were argued, and then a judge pronounced a winner and a loser. The winner stayed on the table, the following challenger was

The Farmer and the Hen: A Lancashire Love Story

placed next to it, and the process was repeated until only one bird was left.[23] The shift in interest from raising fighting birds to showing birds competitively is mirrored in the career of one of the Lancashire pioneers of universal standards, Richard Teebay. At the age of 15 he had owned an unbeaten fighting cock, but in later life had become one of the first judges at national poultry shows.[24]

The first show purely for poultry in England was held either in 1845 in Yorkshire,[25] or in the same year in London,[26] organised by the London Zoo,[27] depending on which authority is to be believed. There was a gap of a year and then the Zoological Society held another more successful one, then the Birmingham Cattle Show added a poultry section in 1848, and thirdly in 1868 the Crystal Palace show started and became acknowledged as the most important of these three winter classics.[28]

At first, poultry shows relied on a limited team of acknowledged experts as judges: J. Dixon, E. Hewitt, R. Teebay, W. B. Tegetmeier, and one or two others.[29] They were answerable only to themselves and their

Fig. 1.7 A rather severe-looking Richard Teebay

The National Background

word was law, and frequently they exhibited considerable enmity towards each other.[30] To show poultry competitively there had to be agreed standards as to what made a prize-winning bird. Each area before that had its own standard,[31] but with the increase in shows and exhibitions across the nation there was a need for some uniformity in the perception of what constituted quality in a breed so that judges could apply the same standards throughout.

The Poultry Club was formed in 1863, and though it lasted for only three years as the hierarchy could not agree,[32] it did produce the first authoritative list of qualities that breeders should aspire to, *The Standard of Excellence in Exhibition Poultry*. Birds were divided into their component parts: comb, beak, head, eye, deaf ear, wattles, neck, back, wings, tail, breast, thighs, fluff, legs, toes and carriage.[33] So, for instance, the Cochin hen's comb should be "Single, very small, low in front, erect and perfectly straight; with small, well-defined serrations."[34] These standards were the work of the aforementioned Dixon, Teebay and Tegetmeier, and aroused some controversy; further revisions occurred until in 1901 a Standards Committee produced a pocket book which coordinated the standards used by specialist breed clubs.[35]

Exhibitions were something of a double-edged sword in the improvement of strains of poultry: they encouraged uniformity in what was desirable among each of the different breeds and suggested the benefits of selective breeding, and they also introduced and popularised new breeds, the Brahma and Cochin in the 1850s, the Plymouth Rock and the Wyandotte in the 1880s.[36] On the other hand they still concentrated on the appearance of the birds and not the economic benefits. Surgeon, painter and poultry fancier Sir Henry Thompson observed in the *Livestock Journal* in 1885: "the poultry fancy of the day, with very little exception, is an unreasoning competition in a keenly contested race for the production not of meat or of eggs but of feathers."[37] Another commentator was equally forthright: "all breeds of birds most desirable for chickens and eggs have had their usefulness destroyed by the fancy breeders who breed birds for exhibition purposes only."[38] "Usefulness" was the key word for the farmer, and so the notion of "Utility Poultry" developed.

A Gender Divide

Breeding therefore came to be regarded more as a science as owners attempted to refine the features of a chick accepted as desirable, and science was seen to be a male discipline, so the gender shift from women to men was given a little further momentum,[39] but it is probable that up until the Great War raising poultry remained largely characterised by a gender divide. Cock fighting and exhibiting competitively were both interests pursued mainly by men; the women looked after the domestic birds about the yard. The prize list for hens and bantams at the London

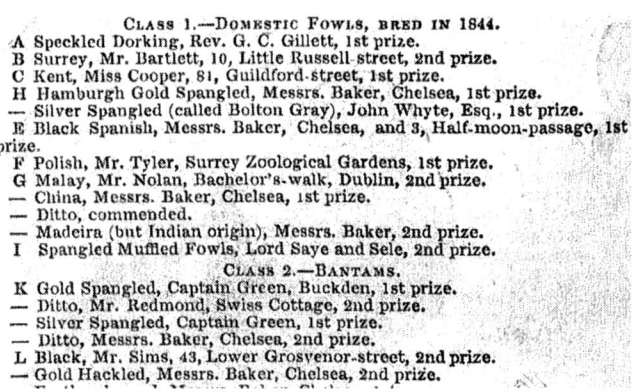

Fig. 1.8 Miss Cooper, 1st prize. Probably Lucy Anne Cooper; the Coopers were solicitors and auctioneers in Russell Square, London. Lucy Anne's brother, William Durrant Cooper, was also a journalist and prolific writer on the history of Sussex and other topics.

show indicates that men were at least the nominal winners, with the honourable exception of Miss Cooper of Guildford Street.

Women remained in charge of the domestic chickens which provided eggs and meat for the family table, a part of farming life not seen as part of the farm's legitimate business, and this situation continued until well into the twentieth century.[40] The Reverend Sturges in 1907 observed, "the average farmer looks upon his poultry as a minor sort of bye-product [sic], a negligible quantity about which he need not bother his head."[41] Some early "experts" were adamant there was no living to be made out of poultry. Lewis Wright could not think of a successful poultry farm in England, and doubted chickens had the constitution to survive when concentrated together in cabins with wooden floors.[42] Sir Walter Gilbey, in a rather bad-tempered review of the state of the industry in 1904, asserted, "It is difficult to account for the belief still entertained by many persons that poultry farms can be made to pay."[43] But another Knight of the Realm thought differently; Sir Edward Brown suggested that men at last saw poultry as a business opportunity: "More recently there has been a tendency to take up this branch of animal husbandry on more extensive lines and as a business worthy their attention [sic], one that has grown in Britain very rapidly."[44]

From Hobby to Profit

Interest in the possibilities of poultry farming was stimulated as farmers felt the need to look elsewhere beyond traditional crops to find products which could turn a profit. Economic factors caused farmers to look for alternatives to arable crops in the latter part of the nineteenth century. Agricultural depression also encouraged farmers to become better businessmen and technically more efficient farmers, and caused many farmers and labourers to give up farming, often to be replaced by more innovative people less bound by tradition.[45] During the second half of the nineteenth century, a succession of poor harvests and the opening up of alternative sources of supply, particularly wheat from North America, had brought difficulties for arable farmers; also industrial areas were emerging as potential markets for different sorts of goods, particularly perishables, and their growing populations represented growing spending power. Those same areas were within easier reach because of the development of the rail network, and there was also government concern at the growing import of eggs from foreign countries.[46] The initial reluctance to consider poultry as a possible source of profit was reinforced by a sort of snobbery: hens were low status; they were the hobby of the women of the house or were for recreation, they were outside the farm economy as generally they foraged for most of their food, and eggs were sold locally, cheaply, and with no concern given to marketing.[47] Male farmers' opposition was gradually overcome as they came to realise the profits poultry could make, and also that poultry could be added to a farm's stock with little disruption to the existing output.

Hens require some regular attention for daily feeding and egg collection, but if they are distributed around the farm no other crop or stock need be displaced, and they can be kept on pasture, arable land or orchard; they also obtain much of their food themselves, and houses and other equipment can be basic, and so if farmed in this non-intensive way, even allowing for a winter drop in egg production, returns are good for very little output.[48] Experts suggested hens could be combined with other products: about 100 per acre on pasture used for grazing stock; 200 per acre on orchards, and fruit and hens were believed to be a profitable combination, though the hens should not be allowed to gorge on fallen fruit.[49] Under a semi-intensive system with runs, Broomhead thought that 400 hens per acre was possible, and even so large a number could be combined with market gardening as hens destroy parasites and fertilise the land before the vegetables are planted.[50]

Other factors contributed to make poultry a viable proposition. In more isolated areas "higglers," local travelling traders, could do business for the farmer, usually for a commission of one or two eggs for each shillingsworth, though the infrequency of visits might mean a delay of up to two weeks before eggs went to market.[51] Railway companies gave concessionary fares for live and dead poultry, and eggs, often up to half price. What was needed next was a more effective distribution system, where eggs could be regularly collected, graded and tested and then sent to markets. Marketing should involve cleaning, packaging, and grading according to size and colour, and to ensure a regular supply farmers should concentrate on improving laying in winter.[52] Marketing issues will be looked at later.

Poultry as a Science

As farmers realised the need to diversify agricultural production from about the second half of the nineteenth century, there was also a growing understanding of the need to put agriculture in general on a more scientific basis if the burgeoning population was to be fed, and if British agriculture was to be able to compete with the opening up of alternative sources of food such as the USA. In the early nineteenth century, usually it was the landlords who had been at the centre of improvements and innovation. From the 1890s research was Government sponsored, through the county councils, and in that same decade societies such as the National Poultry Organisation (1898) were formed.[53] New departments of agriculture in universities, the Royal Agricultural College at Cirencester, and farm institutes created by county councils gradually took over the functions of research and development.[54] By 1914 there were 15 institutions in England, Wales and Scotland offering courses in agriculture to degree level.[55] A number of county councils had appointed organisers of agriculture to provide a link between farmers and the staff of farm schools and colleges, though at first there was some distrust from farmers of men who had only scientific training, and there was also an unwillingness to support the colleges as they were funded from the rates and in rural areas obviously these were paid by farmers.[56]

The Chicken House

The first features of poultry farming to be looked at were housing and feeding. Early poultry books offered free and detailed advice about housing, usually on principles that sheds should be secure, waterproof and draught-free, yet airy. The floor should be dry, and may have on it husks, straw, peat moss or road sweepings, or it could be simply dry earth. Whatever the covering, it should be cleaned occasionally. The hens should have perches available, and the Americans introduced dropping boards under the perches for ease of cleaning, which gradually came into general use in Britain. Somewhere in the shed, and certainly in a dry

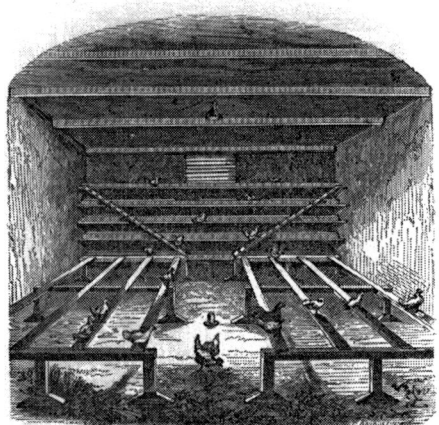

Fig. 1.9 The inside of an ideal hen house c. 1869. They were elaborate and roomy – a far cry from the battery cages of the mid-twentieth century.

place, should be a dust bath of dry earth or ashes for the hen to dust itself and help to reduce parasites. There should be nest boxes on the end walls, feeding troughs and water on the front walls. If the hens are not to range freely, then ideally they should have access to a grass run.[57]

Before proprietary feeds were available the poultry farmer had to provide the feed, and again the benefits of various foodstuffs caused considerable debate. Various combinations of bran, wheat, oats, barley, Indian corn, fresh vegetables, chopped meat, rice, beans and peas were suggested, depending on how much access the hens had to land on which to forage.[58]

The Incubator

Another development towards the end of the nineteenth century was that artificial incubation eventually became practical. The first known experiment was by Cornelis Drebbel from the Netherlands. In 1609 he invented the "Athenor," a coal-fuelled cabinet in which the hot air circulated around an inner box containing eggs. Later, a Frenchman, René Reamur, placed eggs in wooden casks and surrounded them with fermenting dung which was renewed when necessary: "For obvious reasons, this system is never likely to be popular," remarked Lewis Wright, laconically.[59] In 1850, another Frenchman, Cantello, exhibited an incubator based on a hot water system, and though it worked reasonably successfully, there was not at the time sufficient demand for it to be marketed.[60] Others based on copper cisterns or boilers followed, invented by M. Carbonnier, Mr Brindley and F. H. Schroder,[61] but in 1867 Wright concluded firmly that he did not think artificial incubation would ever supplant, commercially, the natural process.[62]

Development seems to have stagnated for a while, and then a Mr Henry Boyle of Ambleside produced an incubator, based again on hot water, but which also circulated air and moisture through the egg

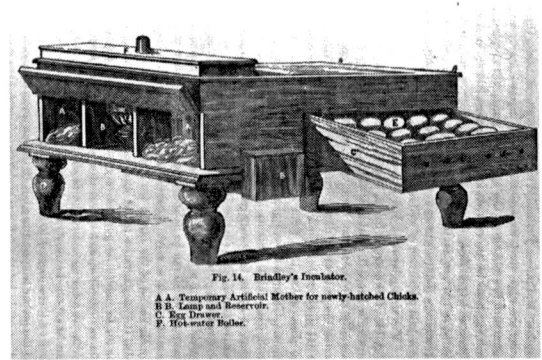

Fig. 1.10 Mr Brindley's incubator. A hot water incubator.

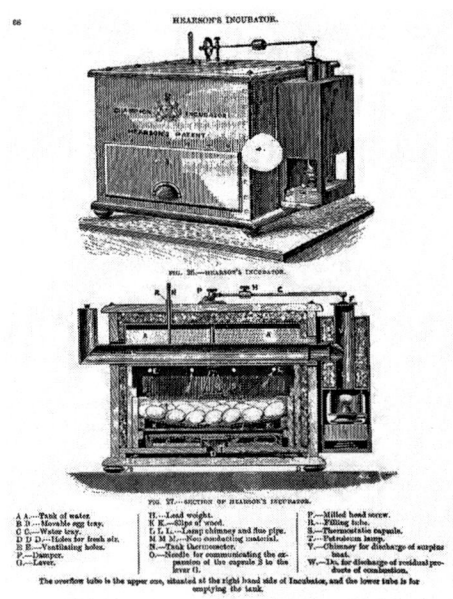

Fig. 1.11 The Hearson incubator

chamber. Unfortunately, the machine was complicated, it held only 24 eggs and cost £45, and the eggs frequently broke. Other subsequent machines such as "The Penman" and the "Hydro-Incubator" had their champions and their faults, but the first practical and reliable machine was the "Hearson Incubator."[63] Taking the broody hen out of the equation had many advantages: a machine with a capacity of 100 eggs could do the work of eight hens, without any worries as to reliability or seasonal variation; there was control over egg selection, and so the flock was improved.[64]

The Hearson incubators were in widespread use from about 1881, until superseded by the "Gloucester" and "Glevum" incubators, both made by two joiner brothers from Dursley in Gloucestershire,[65] and shown later in the section on the Collinson farm.

The Brooder

Artificial incubation enabled a greater quantity of chickens to be produced, and this increase could not be supported without non-natural systems of rearing the chickens, namely "brooders." An early attempt to combine incubation and rearing, the Cantello incubator of 1851, failed, because the two processes are quite different: rearing takes longer, and young chicks require space and freedom, not just a warm environment.[66] The first effective brooder was created in 1873 by Mrs Frank Cheshire, a breeder who exhibited Brahmas, and there was gradual evolution into a relatively standard design based on a hover and a lamp with a curtain arrangement around the hover.[67] When breeders began producing on a large scale, dedicated brooder cabins were built containing a series of such brooders.[68]

The result of these developments was that some establishments set themselves up as breeders, and other farmers chose not to breed their own chicks but to buy either eggs for hatching, day-old chicks or point-of-lay pullets from those breeders, a division which accelerated through

The Farmer and the Hen: A Lancashire Love Story

Fig. 1.12 Mrs Cheshire's brooder. The frequently abrupt Lewis Wright claimed that the diagram "sufficiently explained" its construction: it doesn't. The roof was a zinc tank of hot water, kept warm by a lamp in the aperture on the right. The frame was wood, lined with fleece, the floor dry earth. The faults were poor circulation of air, and the frequent cleaning necessary.

the next century and became established in the 1920s[69]. Profit margins depended on productivity set against incurred costs, and from the late nineteenth century onwards the ordinary poultry keeper found it more profitable to buy in replacement stock rather than to breed his own.[70]

An article in the *Lancashire Daily Post* in 1931 contrasted the old system of rearing hens with the modern (see Figures 1.13 and 1.14).

The National Background

Figs 1.13 and 1.14 The old and the new way of raising chicks, 1931. The descriptions in the article are a little clearer than the photographs.

A New Breed of Chicken

As hens were bred for eggs and meat rather than for exhibitions, so established breeds declined in popularity and were only kept for ornamental purposes by traditionalists, especially the game birds, and the Dorking, Brahma, Hamburg and Cochin. At a meeting of the farmers of Garstang in 1918, Tom Barron (of whom much more later) asserted authoritatively, "the old-fashioned strains were good neither for laying nor for table use."[71] They came to be replaced by larger and more productive breeds, sometimes through evolution of native types, but mostly by breeds from abroad, the Leghorn, Minorca, Wyandotte, Orpington, and Rhode Island Red, from which modern poultry hybrids are descended.[72]

National Initiatives

A further national stimulus to poultry producers, referred to earlier, was the country's reliance on imports and the adverse effect on the balance of payments. In 1896 the value of eggs coming through British ports was £4,184,567.[73] If home production was to be increased, then the emphasis of breeders needed to be on producing heavy layers. A response was the formation of the National Poultry Organisation Society (NPOS), whose aim was to promote poultry keeping in rural districts, improve breeds and management, and attempt to organise a system of marketing to obtain best prices for eggs and poultry.[74] One of the initiatives of the NPOS was to send out a missionary expedition to the Celtic Fringe of England and Wales, which was deemed rather backward in poultry appreciation, in the form of the "Egg Train," or rather more irreverently, the "Omelette Express."

Fig. 1.15 The Egg Train, as featured in the *Western Gazette* in July 1915. Not all articles were so respectful – it was generally greeted by the newspapers with varying levels of amusement.

The National Background

Performance Recording and Testing

The farmers themselves were beginning to appreciate the benefits of identifying the best layers. About this period dairy farmers began to keep records of the milk yields of individual cows, and similar records were adapted for laying hens.[75] Trap nests were invented in America, and they enabled farmers to keep records of the output of identifiably marked or ringed pullets or hens.[76] Trap nests were quite labour intensive in that hens needed to be physically released after laying and the results recorded, but on the individual farms which used them that came to be the job of the youngsters in the family.

Individual farmers monitored their hens; the next step was to compare flocks and breeds on a larger scale. In 1896 the National Utility Poultry Society was founded, and in 1897 its members instituted the first laying trials.[77] Initially these trials were only over 16 weeks, but by 1907–8 they were year-long, divided into 13 groups of 28 days with a short break between tests for administration, and it was shown that winter egg production was an excellent indicator of annual production. Up to 1914–15 all birds were grouped together in trials, but in that year they were divided into breeds, and over the next few years White Leghorns and White Wyandottes proved to be the best layers.[78]

Poultry farmers had great faith in the capacity for laying trials to effect improvements. Jack Wrennall, a leading Lancashire poultryman, speaking to members of the Preston and District Utility Poultry Society in February 1922, informed them that at the first year-long laying trials in 1907–8, the average for the best Leghorns was 141½ eggs per bird. In 1920, in a similar competition, the average for the best pen was 241½ per bird.[79]

The organisation of a laying trial was outlined by Tom Barron when he proposed that the Lancashire Utility Poultry Society should organise their own. There should be at least a hundred pens, which would necessitate

Figs 1.16 and 1.7 National Utility Poultry Society, 1930–1. Awarded to F. W. Barley for six Light Sussex, 1,196 eggs.

a field of at least 6 acres. Fifty poultry houses would need to be built, with each house partitioned into at least two, and each partition should contain separate pens. Each lot of birds should have a run 10 yards by 25 yards. He even proposed building houses for the manager of the scheme and his assistant, something which he frequently did for his workers, as will be shown later. The money for this, £4,000, was to be raised by the members of the Society, and Mr Barron envisaged that all loans would be repaid after five years as the investment was "as sound as the Bank of England."[80]

The first trial was reported at length in the local paper. The hen houses were designed and donated by Jonathan Collinson, the feeders were "Bartle" dry mash hoppers designed by Jack Wrennall, and the floor of the houses was also one of Mr Wrennall's design and apparently much copied by other poultry keepers: a bed of cinders three inches deep was prepared and then a mixture of cinders and cement was laid on it and compressed. This bed was deemed to be both dry and porous.[81]

The National Background

The rules for the Society's second "International Egg-Laying Test 1923–4" are among the papers left to the family of Jonathan Collinson and donated to the Fylde Country Life Preservation Society, and show how much more refined they had become from Tom Barron's general principles of just a couple of years earlier. The test ran for 11 months, from 1 November 1923 to 2 October 1924. There were four sections: open single bird, light section; open single bird, heavy section; novice breeders' light section; and novice breeders' heavy section. Gold, silver and bronze medals were available in the first two sections, silver and bronze for the novice sections, and first- or second-class certificates would be awarded to all birds which it was deemed merited them. There were also four cups to be held by the winners for a year, and the *Preston Guardian* cup, which the owner of the best layer in any section won outright.[82]

Layers of small eggs tended to lay more, and gradually the size of eggs was recorded as part of the trials as well, and then in 1929 the Lancashire Utility Poultry Society attempted to use the laying trials as a basis for producing a register of cockerels and pullets, in other words, a stud book for chickens.[83] This was only abandoned in 1939 when it was felt that diverting feed purely for laying tests was a luxury that could not be afforded in wartime.[84]

Fig. 1.18 Devon trials, 1933. The "Omelette Express" had obviously achieved some success.

A National Industry

Post-1914 the Ministry of Agriculture became more active in instruction and research[85] as the circumstances of war brought home to people how dependent the country was on foreign imports. During the First World War and afterwards research into animal nutritional requirements had brought improved and specialised foodstuffs. T. B. Wood, Professor of Agriculture at Cambridge University, published *Composition and Nutritive Value of Feedstuffs* (1918) and *Animal Nutrition* (1924), and by the mid-1920s corn merchants were providing complete feeds for sows, milk cattle, beef cattle, fattening pigs, and for day-old chicks and laying hens.[86] Specific animal research tended to be funded by government grants and by support from specialised rather than general farmers. The Lancashire poultry farmers, for instance, supported the National Poultry Institute.[87]

Further Research and Development

After the First World War there was greater willingness to accept expert advice as the war had resulted in greater contact between farmers and the staff of agricultural schools and colleges, as those staff had often also been employees of county committees or officers of the Food Production Department. Farmers were compelled to listen to these experts, as their findings might result in subsequent cultivation orders.[88] There was a consequent increase in the desire of interested parties to bond together to protect their interests: by the end of the war, for example, the National Farmers' Union (NFU) claimed 80,000 members in 58 county branches.[89]

Gradually the results of the research permeated down into farming practice. Agricultural economists persuaded farmers to supply information on costs, investments and incomes, and found that profits were firmly linked with high output per man, per acre and per unit of capital, and that dairy cows, pigs and poultry yielded more than beef cattle and sheep, while vegetables and sugar beet gave more profit than turnips and swedes.[90]

Thus the poultry industry developed alongside, and in many ways because of, a growing interest in the economic and scientific analysis of what worked best in agriculture. The best designs for poultry housing were established. The results of egg-laying trials gave poultry farmers statistical information to add to the vague conclusions gathered by the few farmers who had bothered to keep some records, and to accepted folk practice.[91] Research into what nutrients laying chickens required led to improvements in feed, and commercial feed producers were already in existence to supply the dairy industry.[92] Some problems remained, but even the problem of having to rear unwanted cockerels until their sex could be determined was in the process of being solved by 1930 with genetic developments which enabled differentiation by colour and markings.[93]

The Economics of Poultry Farming

Economic analysis revolved around selling price set against cost of production, and supply and demand. Dr A. C. Ruston, lecturer in Agricultural Economics at Leeds University, spelt that out to a meeting of the Lancashire Utility Poultry Society in the Scientific Meeting Rooms in Preston in February 1926, and identified eggs as the only agricultural product for which demand had exceeded supply in every year since 1920. Lancashire in particular seemed aware of this as an opportunity; it was the only county which in 1921 had more poultry than it had in 1913[94]. Dr Ruston divided investment into livestock, i.e. the birds, and "deadstock", the equipment needed to house and maintain them. Livestock made money, but as the latter suffered from depreciation and so on, that was the area where costs should be kept to a minimum. A further way of reducing costs was when labour was done by members of the family or the farmer himself, which in central Lancashire was the dominant way that farming was organised. Dr Ruston's main point was that farmers should not treat accounts as a necessary chore, but should "look into them, and make them tell the story they could be made to tell."[95] Certainly labour was a major consideration when a farmer considered the method of poultry farming to be used: under a semi-intensive system, one observer reckoned, one man could look after 1,250 birds.[96]

Free Range versus Intensive

Closer focus on the economics of poultry farming led to experiments with different ways of organising the stock and the possibilities and drawbacks of each. E. T. Brown summarised the main methods that had been established by the 1930s. Though there were variations within these broad bands, he listed four main methods: free range, semi-intensive, intensive and battery.[97] "Free range," as the name suggests, allows the hens to roam freely from their relatively isolated houses. Relatively few birds were kept per acre, between 25 and 50. "Semi-intensive" covers a range of alternatives, but basically the hens are kept in cabins with peat moss ("deep litter") or chopped straw or shavings on the floor, with access to enclosed runs.[98] The average number of birds per acre was between 300 and 400.[99] Under the "intensive" system birds are confined in their cabins from the moment they start to lay: because a lot of hens are kept together great attention has to be paid to cleanliness, to minimise the risk of diseases, and dietary requirements, as there is no access to natural food, but the method proved successful on farms with a limited amount of space.

Manufacturers adopted the nomenclature (see Figure 1.9).

The intensive system was initially called "The City System." It was developed in the United States and appeared for the first time in Britain at the Festival of Empire held at the Crystal Palace in 1911.[100]

The National Background

Fig. 1.19 An advertisement from a poultry manual. Manufacturers realised the value of adaptable buildings, and in this case even claimed the catalogue was a work of art.

Mrs M. Baynes, an early supporter, outlined the advantages as a greater number of birds could be kept per acre than in free range or semi-intensive systems, and egg production per bird was higher.[101] She advocated a minimum of 3 square feet per bird. [102]

The battery system was the brainchild of a Mr Few of Somerset in the 1930s.[103] At first this was used as a way of rearing chicks from one day to 10-to-12 weeks old in a controlled environment, and then after a short period of acclimatisation the birds were moved to "night arks."[104] When Brown was writing in 1934 the system was still in its infancy but had been adapted to laying hens. Birds were kept in tiered cages with tightly controlled lighting and ventilation, with feeding and cleaning made as mechanical as possible so that a minimum of attention was required.[105] The perceived advantages were outlined in an article in the Lancashire Utility Poultry Society (LUPS) Yearbook of 1936: poor layers could be quickly identified and culled, birds were kept away from their droppings so the chances of disease were reduced, and as the environment was controlled the overseer of the poultry could organise his/her time. It was estimated that one man working a 48-hour week could look after 1,500 birds. Birds of different ages could be kept in the same cabin and so the cabin kept at full capacity.[106]

An article in the LUPS yearbook of the year before had attempted to refute criticisms of the battery system, answering objections on the grounds of cruelty, poor shells and high numbers of casualties,[107] and claiming that if the only issue was food cost, then battery farming was the most economical. In a paper presented to the Annual Poultry Conference at Harper Adams College, H. E. Swepstone had calculated the amount of food needed to produce a dozen eggs under the different systems:

Semi-intensive	7 lb 4 oz
Intensive	7 lb 6 oz
Battery	6 lb 15 oz[108]

The battery system was banned in Britain in January 2012.

A more detailed description of the types of poultry keepers was in a Ministry of Agriculture report of 1926 which classified the producers of poultry and eggs in seven ways. This lists the types of poultry farmer

The National Background

still found today, irrespective of whether the holding is organised on free range, semi-intensive or intensive lines:

1. The small producer, often a country cottager or town back-yarder
2. The smallholder, often reliant on poultry for his livelihood
3. The general farmer, with a few poultry as a side-line
4. The commercial egg farm
5. The specialist rearer of chickens or ducklings for fattening
6. The specialist fattener, who buys young birds from breeders or rearers
7. The specialist breeder who sells eggs, chickens and adult birds for stock[109]

Night Lights

Three more aspects which affected poultry keeping as a whole might be mentioned before moving on to focus on the particular region in question. Whatever the system of farming, further improvement in laying output came with the increase in artificial lighting: a big disadvantage of the British poultry industry in competing with foreign imports was the decline in productivity during the dark winter months, when because of this decline egg prices were at their highest. The effect of artificial lighting is to lengthen the hen's working day to between 12 and 14 hours.[110] The first countries to introduce lighting were the USA and Denmark, and by the 1920s it was in general use in America among commercial egg farmers.[111] The Lancashire County Farm at Hutton, Preston, experimented with artificial lighting over several years and in 1926 concluded that artificial lighting meant an extra profit of 1s. 6d. per bird over the months between October and January.[112] Initially lighting took the form of paraffin lamps and carbide lamps, which were quite labour intensive as lamps needed to be trimmed and fuel topped up, and they needed to be physically lit, but by the 1930s electricity was becoming available even to farm outbuildings and timing switches made the operation an easy one. Any debate as to which source of power was best was effectively over: in 1931, Tom Elliott, Tom Barron's business associate[113] and later in charge of the National Laying Test at Godalming in Surrey, asserted assuredly: "incubation, brooding, and, on a commercial farm, lighting up can now in most districts be done much better and cheaper with electricity."[114]

Disease Control

Disease is still a concern for the modern poultry farmer. As systems of poultry farming grew more intensive, so disease became more of a problem. The LUPS books chart something of the poultry farmers' worries about illnesses and the measures being taken to combat the various afflictions birds suffered. Many, such as coccidiosis, bumble foot, fowl pest and infectious laryngotracheitis (ILT), are still with us, though preventive treatment has improved over the years, and some of them, especially bacillary white diarrhoea (BWD), have been virtually eradicated by careful blood testing of stock. Interestingly, Newcastle disease (fowl pest), the poultry farmer's scourge in the 1950s and 60s, was a relatively late arrival. An article in the *Preston Guardian* in 1927 speaks of a "new poultry malady," the first outbreak of which was in the Newcastle area; mortality was noted as virtually 100%, though incidence of the disease was at the time rare.[115] By the 1960s, heaps of soil indicating where infected slaughtered birds lay were features of most poultry farms.

Marketing

A Ministry report into the marketing of eggs in 1927 identified several problems: there was "free inflow" of eggs from countries which produced a surplus of eggs, and though the standard of our own eggs was improving, so was the standard of the exporting countries,

The National Background

Fig. 1.20 A fowl pest burial in Pilling in the 1960s. Fowl pest heaps were a depressingly familiar part of the Fylde landscape at this time. The men from the Ministry came in the night and gassed the flocks while the hens were roosting. The carcases were then buried.

particularly nearby countries such as Ireland, Holland, Denmark and Belgium, and their eggs achieved better prices than ungraded British eggs in the London market. NFU members observed eggs being unloaded at Liverpool from as far away as Chile and China, and wanted these, and Chinese liquid eggs, used in the catering and confectionery industries, stopped.[116] So the marketing problem, as outlined in the report, basically came down to a need to improve the consistency in the quality of the eggs, but more importantly to improve the preparation of produce for sale.[117] Poultry farmers also felt the Government should control the importation of lower-grade eggs for the catering trade.

Another problem for egg producers was the fluctuation in prices caused by winter scarcity and spring excess. In 1924 the average retail price for eggs in December was 3s. 6d. and in January 3s. 3d. In April, May and June it was 1s. 6d.[118]

The Government did begin to respond to these concerns during the 1930s. After a successful lobby to have foreign eggs stamped with the country of origin, there was a movement towards more central control and the National Egg Mark Scheme was introduced as "the first organised effort to provide the market in quantity with reliably graded English eggs of the highest quality."[119] Then the National Egg Mark Central Ltd was created which aimed to channel eggs in times of surplus to areas where they were needed.[120] One less piecemeal solution to this would have been to strengthen state control by establishing an egg marketing board, a producer–Government alliance which could determine standards and distribution and set prices nationally. By September 1933, Mr J. Hill, chairman of the Lancashire Branch of the NFU, was confident enough to suggest one would be ready in ten months and members should prepare for its inception and wherever possible should establish producer-controlled egg-packing stations.[121] Any proposed scheme, however, foundered on the matter of import controls: by March 1937 the County Poultry Committee was reporting that Lancashire's poultry farmers were in serious difficulties because of increasing imports, a fall in egg prices and increased feed costs. They urged the Government to take special measures to protect the industry, particularly with higher tariffs on imported eggs,[122] but the Government was reluctant to comply. The Egg Marketing Board did not come into existence until December 1956.

So far, national factors behind the development of the British poultry industry have been suggested, and several references made specifically to mid-Lancashire and its leading poultry men and associations. It is now time to focus more specifically on that one area, and to look at the local dynamics which enabled the industry to flourish.

The National Background

Notes

1 Fred Hams, *Old Poultry Breeds* (Princes Risborough. Shire, 2004), p. 4.
2 Sir Edward Brown, *British Poultry Husbandry: Its Evolution and History* (London: Chapman and Hall's, 1930 [Read Books facsimile, August 2010]), pp. 37–41. Brown cites Gervase Markham's book, *Cheape and Goode Husbandry* (1614), as debating what made a good cock.
3 Sir Walter Gilbey, *Sport in the Olden Time* (London. Vinton and Co., 1912), p. 11.
4 Herbert Atkinson, *The Old English Game Fowl: Its History, Description, Management and Feeding* (London. The Fanciers' Gazette, 1891), pp. 43–4.
5 Atkinson, *Old English Game Fowl*, p. 28.
6 Atkinson, *Old English Game Fowl*, pp. 55–6.
7 Gilbey, *Sport in the Olden Time*, p. 57.
8 Gilbey, *Sport in the Olden Time*, p. 59.
9 Stephen K. Halliwell, *Preston Pubs* (Stroud, Gloucestershire. Amberley Publishing, 2014).
10 H. Easom Smith, *Modern Poultry Development* (Liss, Hampshire. Spur Publications, 1976), p. 7.
11 George Beesley, *A Report of the State of Agriculture in Lancashire, with Observations on the Political Position and General Prospects of the Agricultural Classes* (Preston. Dobson and Son, 1849).
12 Sir Edward Brown, *Memories at Eventide* (Burnley, Lancashire. John Dixon, 1934), pp. 42–3.
13 Sir Walter Gilbey, *Farm Stock of Old* (Liss, Hampshire. Spur Publications, 1976), p. 129. Originally published as *Farm Stock 100 Years Ago* (1910).
14 J. Stephen Hicks, *The Possibilities of Modern Poultry Keeping* (London. The Cable Printing and Publishing Company, 1909), pp. 30–1.
15 Hams, *Old Poultry Breeds*, p. 8.
16 Andrew Lawler, *Why Did the Chicken Cross the World?* (London. Duckworth Overlook, 2015), pp. 120–2.
17 Brown, *British Poultry Husbandry*, pp. 84–5.
18 Easom Smith, *Modern Poultry Development*, p. 20.
19 L. Wright, *The Practical Poultry Keeper: A Complete and Standard Guide to the Management of Poultry* (New York. Orange Judd Co., 1894), pp. 141–2.
20 Brown, *British Poultry Husbandry*, p. 85.

21   Hams, *Old Poultry Breeds*, p. 9.
22   *Cottage Gardener*, 23 December 1852, quoted by Brown, *British Poultry Husbandry*, p. 81.
23   "Mr Richard Teebay," *Preston Guardian*, 13 September 1879, p. 2.
24   "Mr Richard Teebay," *Preston Guardian*, 13 September 1879, p. 2.
25   Brown, *British Poultry Husbandry*, p. 12.
26   Brown, *British Poultry Husbandry*, p. 81. Brown cites both venues as the first at different points in his book. Certainly the London show was not a financial success and only ran for the one year.
27   Easom Smith, *Modern Poultry Development*, p. 13
28   Easom Smith, *Modern Poultry Development*, pp. 14–15.
29   Easom Smith, *Modern Poultry Development*, p. 34.
30   Easom Smith, *Modern Poultry Development*, pp. 34–5.
31   Brown, *British Poultry Husbandry*, p. 79.
32   Easom Smith, *Modern Poultry Development*, p. 35.
33   The Poultry Club, *The Standard of Excellence in Exhibition Poultry* (London. The Poultry Club, published by Groombridge and Sons, 1865), p. 6.
34   The Poultry Club, *Standard of Excellence in Exhibition Poultry*, p. 6.
35   Easom Smith, *Modern Poultry Development*, p. 35.
36   Brown, *British Poultry Husbandry*, p. 158.
37   Sir Henry Thompson, *The Livestock Journal*, 27 February 1885, quoted in Brown, *British Poultry Husbandry*, p. 150.
38   Sir Walter Gilbey, *Poultry-Keeping on Farms and Small Holdings* (London. Vinton and Co., 1904), p. 7.
39   Brown, *British Poultry Husbandry*, p. 89.
40   Christabel S. Orwin and Edith H. Whetham, *History of British Agriculture: 1846–1914* (Newton Abbot. David and Charles, 1971), pp. 85–6.
41   Rev. T. W. Sturges, *Poultry Culture for Profit* (London. MacDonald and Evans, 1907), p. 8.
42   L. Wright, *The Practical Poultry Keeper: A Complete and Standard Guide to the Management of Poultry* (London and New York. Cassell, Petter and Galpin, 1867), pp. 221–3.
43   Gilbey, *Poultry-Keeping on Farms and Small Holdings* p. 5.
44   Brown, *British Poultry Husbandry*, p. 22.

The National Background

45   P. J. Perry, *British Agriculture 1875–1914* (London. Methuen and Co., 1973), p. xiii.
46   Brown, *British Poultry Husbandry*, p. 160.
47   Brown, *British Poultry Husbandry*, p. 161.
48   Brown, *British Poultry Husbandry*, pp. 165–6.
49   William W. Broomhead, *Poultry Breeding and Management* (London. New Era Publishing Co. [1937]), pp. 8–9.
50   Broomhead, *Poultry Breeding and Management*, pp. 11–13.
51   Sturges, *Poultry Culture for Profit*, pp. 13–14.
52   Sturges, *Poultry Culture for Profit*, p. 15.
53   Brown, *British Poultry Husbandry*, p. 219.
54   Edith H. Whetham, *The Agrarian History of England and Wales, Vol. VIII: 1914–1939* (Cambridge. Cambridge University Press, 1978), p. 54.
55   Whetham, *Agrarian History of England and Wales, Vol. VIII*, p. 66.
56   Whetham, *Agrarian History of England and Wales, Vol. VIII*, p. 67.
57   Combined advice from two early experts on poultry, Lewis Wright and William M. Lewis. L. Wright, *The Practical Poultry Keeper: A Complete and Standard Guide to the Management of Poultry* (New York. Orange Judd Co., 1894), pp. 1–12; and William M. Lewis, *The People's Practical Poultry Book: A Work on the Breeds, Breeding, Rearing and General Management of Poultry* (New York: The American News Company, 1871), pp. 104–6.
58   A combination of the suggestions of the same two authorities. Wright, *Practical Poultry Keeper*, pp. 18–24, and Lewis, *People's Practical Poultry Book*, pp. 21–2.
59   Wright, *Practical Poultry Keeper*, p. 203.
60   Brown, *British Poultry Husbandry*, p. 189.
61   Wright, *Practical Poultry Keeper*, pp. 203–8.
62   Wright, *Practical Poultry Keeper*, p. 208.
63   Brown, *British Poultry Husbandry*, pp. 190–1.
64   Brown, *British Poultry Husbandry*, p. 192.
65   Thomas E. Whittle, *A Triumph of Science: A 70 Year History of the U.K. Poultry Industry* (self-published [1997]), p. 8.
66   Brown, *British Poultry Husbandry*, p. 196.
67   S. H. Lewer, *Wright's Book of Poultry: Revised and Edited in Accordance with the Latest Poultry Club Standards* (London. Cassell and Co., 1913), pp. 100–3.

68 Brown, *British Poultry Husbandry*, p. 199.
69 "Trading in Chickens: New Developments in the Poultry Industry," *Preston Guardian*, 6 July 1929, p. 10.
70 Brown, *British Poultry Husbandry*, p. 267.
71 "Poultry Management: Mr T. Barron Lectures at Garstang," *Preston Guardian*, 21 September 1918, p. 5.
72 Brown, *British Poultry Husbandry*, p. 265.
73 Brown, *British Poultry Husbandry*, p. 269.
74 Brown, *Memories at Eventide*, pp. 102–3.
75 Brown, *British Poultry Husbandry*, p. 270.
76 Brown, *British Poultry Husbandry*, p. 271.
77 Brown, *British Poultry Husbandry*, p. 271.
78 Brown, *British Poultry Husbandry*, p. 272.
79 "Poultry Lecture: Mr J. Wrennall on Selection and Breeding," *Preston Guardian*, 4 February 1922, p. 2.
80 "Lancashire Poultry Society's Important Scheme," *Preston Guardian*, 24 September 1921, p. 8.
81 "Lancashire's International Egg-Laying Test," *Preston Guardian*, 21 October 1922, p. 6.
82 "The Lancashire Utility Poultry Society: Particulars and Conditions of the Second Annual International Egg-Laying Test – 1923–4." From the papers of Jonathan Collinson held by John Higginson of the Fylde Country Life Preservation Society.
83 Brown, *British Poultry Husbandry*, p. 274.
84 "Introduction by The Secretary," Lancashire Utility Poultry Society Yearbook, 1940 (Preston. LUPS. R. Seed, printer), p. 3.
85 Brown, *British Poultry Husbandry*, pp. 224–5.
86 Whetham, *Agrarian History of England and Wales, Vol. VIII*, p. 199.
87 Whetham, *Agrarian History of England and Wales, Vol. VIII*, p. 200.
88 Whetham, *Agrarian History of England and Wales, Vol. VIII*, p. 128.
89 Whetham, *Agrarian History of England and Wales, Vol. VIII*, p. 129.
90 Whetham, *Agrarian History of England and Wales, Vol. VIII*, p. 222.
91 W. W. Gardner, "Artificial Lighting for Egg Production," Lancashire Utility Poultry Society Yearbook, 1930 (Preston. LUPS. R. Seed, printer), p. 57.
92 Perry, *British Agriculture 1875–1914*, p. 82.
93 Whetham, *Agrarian History of England and Wales, Vol. VIII*, p. 221.

94 "Poultry Problems: How Profits May Vanish," *Preston Guardian*, 27 February 1926, p. 15.
95 "Poultry Problems: How Profits May Vanish," p. 15.
96 "Poultry Industry: Impressions of Lancashire's Enterprise," *Preston Guardian*, 16 July 1927, p. 7.
97 E. T. Brown, *The Poultry Keeper's Text Book* (London. Ward Lock and Co., 1924), p. 77.
98 Brown, *Poultry Keeper's Text Book*, pp. 78–82.
99 T. Newman, "The Intensive System of Poultry Keeping," Lancashire Utility Poultry Society Yearbook, 1930 (Preston. LUPS. R. Seed, printer), p. 35.
100 S. H. Lewer, "Intensive and Semi-Intensive Poultry-Keeping," in Lewer, *Wright's Book of Poultry*, p. v.
101 M. Baynes, *Intensive Poultry Culture* (London. The Feathered World, 3rd edition, 1916), p. 9.
102 Baynes, *Intensive Poultry Culture*, p. 17.
103 Whittle, *A Triumph of Science*, p. 22.
104 "Profitable Poultry: Rearing Chicks by the Battery System," *Sussex Agricultural Express*, 30 January 1931, p. 13.
105 Brown, *Poultry Keeper's Text Book*, p. 82.
106 T. Simpson, "Single-Hen Batteries," Lancashire Utility Poultry Society Yearbook, 1936 (Preston. LUPS. R. Seed, printer), p. 47.
107 Major H. C. Few, "Laying Batteries," Lancashire Utility Poultry Society Yearbook, 1935 (Preston. LUPS. R. Seed, printer), p. 67.
108 H. E. Swepstone, "Some Points in Connection with Laying Batteries," Lancashire Utility Poultry Society Yearbook, 1937 (Preston. LUPS. R. Seed, printer), p. 31.
109 Ministry of Agriculture and Fisheries, *Report on the Marketing of Poultry in England and Wales* (London. HMSO, 1927), p. 1.
110 R. Borlase Matthews, "Electric Light on the Poultry Farm," Lancashire Utility Poultry Society Yearbook, 1934 (Preston. LUPS. R. Seed, printer), p. 73.
111 "American Scientist's Visit to Lancashire," *Preston Guardian*, 20 August 1921, p. 2.
112 "County Farm: Record Gathering on Open Day," *Preston Guardian*, 11 September 1926, p. 14.
113 "Laying Stock: Pure and Cross-Bred Birds Contrasted," *Preston Guardian*, 15 December 1928, p. 10.

114 Tom Elliott, "Commercial v. Pedigree Poultry Keeping," Lancashire Utility Poultry Society Yearbook, 1931 (Preston. LUPS. R. Seed, printer), p. 59.
115 "New Poultry Malady," *Preston Guardian*, 27 August 1927, p. 10.
116 LRO DDX 1706/3/5 Lancashire Branch of the NFU, Executive Committee Minute Book 1933–1938, Executive Committee, 27 January 1934.
117 Ministry of Agriculture and Fisheries, *Report on the Marketing of Poultry in England and Wales*, pp. 19–21.
118 Ministry of Agriculture and Fisheries, *Report on the Marketing of Poultry in England and Wales*, p. 18.
119 Ministry of Agriculture and Fisheries, *Eggs and Poultry: Report of the Reorganisation Commission for Great Britain* (London. HMSO, 1935), p. 22.
120 Ministry of Agriculture and Fisheries, *Eggs and Poultry*, p. 23.
121 LRO DDX 1706/3/5 Lancashire Branch of the NFU, Executive Committee Minute Book 1933–1938, Executive Committee, 2 September 1933.
122 LRO DDX 1706/3/5 Lancashire Branch of the NFU, Executive Committee Minute Book 1933–1938, Executive Committee, 6 March 1

2

THE MID-LANCASHIRE POULTRY INDUSTRY

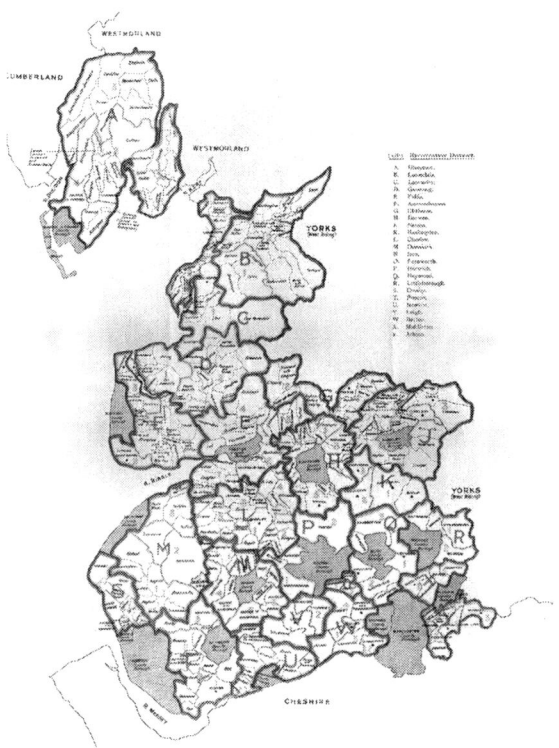

Fig. 2.1 Lancashire (excluding Furness), 1937 (pre-Local Government Act 1972). Larger towns are shaded.

The Farmer and the Hen: A Lancashire Love Story

Competitive Breeding

From its incipient days the poultry industry was associated with Lancashire. The only areas of Britain to compete with Lancashire in poultry breeding were west Yorkshire and the south-east of England. All three were characterised by proximity to industrial districts and urban populations, while Lancashire also had a high proportion of smallholdings which lent themselves to chicken rearing, and there was a tradition of interest in poultry raising even from the time when cock fighting was legal: the Earls of Derby gave their name to a breed of black reds,[1] and Lord Derby and cock fighting were both popular features of the Preston Guild of 1802.

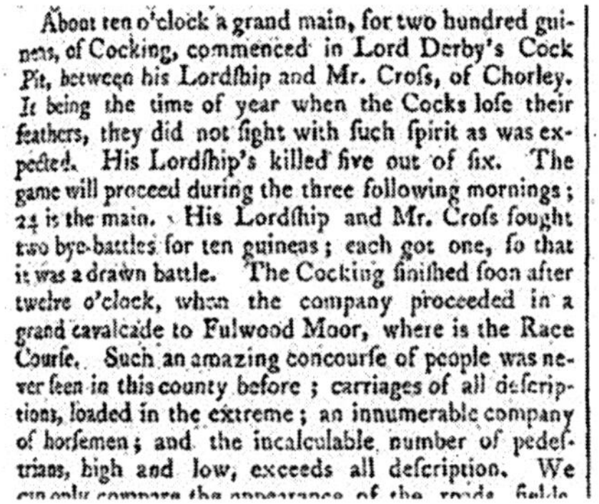

> About ten o'clock a grand main, for two hundred guineas, of Cocking, commenced in Lord Derby's Cock Pit, between his Lordship and Mr. Crofs, of Chorley. It being the time of year when the Cocks lofe their feathers, they did not fight with fuch fpirit as was expected. His Lordship's killed five out of fix. The game will proceed during the three following mornings; 21 is the main. His Lordship and Mr. Crofs fought two bye-battles for ten guineas; each got one, fo that it was a drawn battle. The Cocking finished foon after twelve o'clock, when the company proceeded in a grand cavalcade to Fulwood Moor, where is the Race Courfe. Such an amazing concourfe of people was never feen in this county before; carriages of all defcriptions, loaded in the extreme; an innumerable company of horfemen; and the incalculable number of pedeftrians, high and low, exceeds all defcription. We can only compare the appearance of the roads, fields

Fig. 2.2 Cock fighting as part of the Preston Guild celebrations. A "main" was simply the name for a cock-fighting contest, though a "Welsh Main" was like the quarter finals of a cup competition; eight birds fought one-to-one contests on a knockout basis until one winner remained.

So the area seems always to have had an affinity with fowls. Even when cock fighting declined, the interest in breeding continued: competitive focus turned towards the shows and exhibitions which many towns and villages ran.

Early Birds

Interest in poultry was, for a long time, small scale and localised, but was occasionally considered noteworthy. In 1702 Thomas Sulief travelled around the north of England, and praised the appearance and eggs of what he called "Black Pheasants," which were probably, according to L. Frank Baum, Black Hamburgs.[2] But even by 1882, poultry had made little impact on the agricultural economy of Lancashire. Mr Coleman's Report to the Royal Commission on Agriculture of that year made no mention at all of poultry.[3] A commercial poultry farm was launched in the 1880s by Thomas Carr, near Liverpool, but his farm was not a success: the houses were overcrowded, poorly ventilated and difficult to clean, and so disease was rife and losses high.[4] The investment required for specialist equipment and maintenance was not rewarded with greater returns, and it was felt that only breeding farms which could also sell eggs for hatching could survive.[5] Poultry as a hobby did prosper, however, in the rapidly expanding towns of Lancashire and Yorkshire, particularly in the single-mill towns where land was not at a premium and space allowed householders a garden and a patch of land for poultry. The gender gap noted nationally was sharpened here, as breeding was pursued as a hobby by the men of the towns, whereas on the farms poultry keeping was generally the responsibility of the women.[6]

Gradual Recognition

Most farms had some hens which the women could use for "hen money" to pay for household items, and as poultry began to gain recognition as a legitimate form of husbandry, so there was an early association with Lancashire. The first Royal Agricultural Society Show to include a poultry section was held in Preston in 1885; it represented an acknowledgement that poultry could be viewed as profitable livestock,[7] and was also an encouragement to farmers to take up poultry farming.[8] Further encouragement came from published materials. From 1884 the *Preston Guardian* ran a regular poultry column, supplementing the literature available nationally in journals such as the *Fanciers' Gazette* (1874), *Poultry* (1887) and *The Feathered World* (1889),[9] and specialist authors such as W. B. Tegetmeier, Lewis Wright and Edward Brown produced books designed to advise the would-be farmer.[10] In that year for the first time poultry was included in the Agricultural Returns for the County.[11]

The *Preston Guardian* of the following week exhorted the farmers of Lancashire to increase their commitment to poultry farming, for the country as a whole in 1884 had spent £2,732,055 on importing eggs from abroad.[12]

Agricultural Depression – a Boost for Poultry

A report of 1935 notes that, in most industries, a reduction in profits tends to lead to a contraction of production, but with agriculture, the first effect of bad times is to induce greater output at the lower prices in an endeavour to maintain total gross income, which can hasten the failure of the business.[13] An alternative is that when one branch of farming ceases to make a profit, farmers turn to other branches. The generally recognised national agricultural depression of 1885–95 confirmed both these features. Desperately increasing output resulted in the collapse of many large arable farms, and of small farms managed on crop rotations similar to those used on large farms:[14] in Lancashire the farms which weathered the storm tended to be family farms using intensive systems or "high farming" methods, and producing poultry, pigs, fruit, vegetables and early potatoes, particularly where farms had an urban market nearby, so they were not dependent on one specific crop. The relatively small size of the farms of mid-Lancashire also helped them to survive:[15] they tended

	1884. Acres.	1883. Acres.
Total Area	1,207,926	1,207,926
Total Acreage under Crops, Bare Fallow, and Grass	806,204	797,805
Corn Crops:		
Wheat	25,131	22,836
Barley or Bere	8,160	8,418
Oats	65,340	65,182
Rye	1,732	1,625
Beans	2,909	2,933
Peas	358	364
Total Acreage of Corn Crops	103,630	101,358
Green Crops:		
Potatoes	40,828	39,283
Turnips and Swedes	10,457	10,489
Mangold	1,093	1,035
Carrots	544	475
Cabbage, Kohl-Rabi, and Rape	1,825	1,775
Vetches and other Green Crops, except Clover or Grass	3,769	3,270
Total Acreage of Green Crops	58,516	56,327
Clover, Sanfoin, and Grasses under Rotation	64,507	66,712
Permanent Pasture or Grass not broken up in Rotation (exclusive of Heath or Mountain Land)	576,598	570,246
Flax	1	1
Hops	—	—
Bare Fallow or Uncropped Arable Land	2,952	3,161
Horses (including Ponies), as returned by Occupiers of Land:		
Used solely for purpose of Agriculture, &c.	24,107	24,719
Unbroken Horses and Mares kept solely for Breeding	11,930	11,856
Total of Horses	36,037	36,575
Cattle—Cows and Heifers in Milk or in Calf	123,525	121,267
Other Cattle:		
2 Years of Age and Above	27,973	27,238
Under 2 Years of Age	73,983	69,710
Total of Cattle	225,481	218,215
Sheep—1 Year old and above	171,292	159,725
Under 1 Year old	109,472	104,750
Total of Sheep	280,764	264,475
Pigs	48,859	46,986
Poultry:		
Turkeys	5,635	—
Geese	20,646	—
Ducks	59,844	—
Fowls	449,333	—

Fig. 2.3 Lancashire Agricultural Returns, 1884. Low on the list, but poultry features at last.

to be smallholdings of less than 50 acres and family owned. Historians such as Michael Winstanley note that this occasioned a sort of snobbery among commentators as "family farm" became a sort of synonym for "small" and "less market-oriented,"[16] but because of the relatively large contribution of labour by the farmers themselves and their families,[17] cost of labour was a less important expense than on larger arable farms elsewhere.[18] Also, and importantly, in times of economic recession milk, fruit, vegetables and eggs provided a regular and almost instant income through the year, unlike stock rearing which tied up capital until the animals were sold.

Industrial Markets

This particular area had another advantage over other parts of the country at the time. The population of Lancashire increased by approximately 50% between 1867 and 1898, and against the general trend, earnings of the working class in the county were actually increasing: earnings in the Lancashire cotton industry rose by some 25% in that same period at a time when retail prices fell by about 26%.[19] With the rise in income came changes in taste, a preference for protein rather than starch, and for animal products rather than cereals and potatoes.[20] Close proximity to customers meant farmers were not caught up in lengthy distribution chains, and frequently they were producer retailers, and so kept the profits that would otherwise go to wholesalers;[21] they also recognised that their best interests lay with linking themselves to consumer demand rather than with the protectionist policies of the predominantly arable "agricultural interest."[22] These factors were reflected in a further Royal Commission Report in 1894, concentrating on the Garstang area of Lancashire, which revealed that poultry was gradually being woven into a more mixed economy as farmers looked to survive the depression. It was noted as a general comment that "Among some of the smaller farmers rearing poultry and growing fruit is becoming more common."²³ The appendices gave two specific examples: Mr Dobson of Upper Rawcliffe believed he had made £30 from his hens in the previous year,²⁴ and Thomas "Shendly" (a mis-transcription of "Sherdley;" Thomas Sherdley was an innovative farmer who is credited with introducing the Bramley apple into the orchards of the village²⁵) had diversified into sheep, butter and eggs, all of which he sold himself, either directly to the butcher or at the market at Fleetwood.²⁶

Fig. 2.4 Thomas Sherdley's obituary. He was a respected and influential figure in local agricultural circles.

The Influence of the Great War

The Great War highlighted the need for the country to become more self-sufficient in agriculture, and in Lancashire there were opportunities after the war for those with farming ambitions. Wartime restrictions on rents, and then the post-war rise in maintenance costs, meant that landowners were often keen to sell their properties, which could then be bought reasonably cheaply: it has been estimated that about one quarter of all agricultural land in England and Wales changed hands in the first few years after the war.[27] There was also an increase in low-cost publications explaining current thinking in farming matters, and when the agricultural institutions opened up again through 1919 and 1920 many ex-servicemen attended alongside boys straight from school.[28] The Land Settlement Act (1919) established a fund of £20 million to reimburse county councils for providing small holdings for ex-servicemen. Sir Edward Brown even toured the battle areas of north-east France to advocate the benefits of poultry husbandry to soldiers awaiting demob.[29] In Lancashire, 400 returning soldiers applied for land amounting to 6,000 acres in total, and the take-up in central Lancashire was especially high.[30] By 1925 the Lancashire Agricultural Commission was reporting to Lancashire County Council that 352 small holdings had been created after the act, in addition to the 71 before it, and though 47 tenants had given up their holdings, only four had done so because of financial problems.[31] Nationally, almost 17,000 tenants were eventually settled on over 250,000 acres as the Government honoured its pledges to provide land for those ex-servicemen who wanted it, to provide more employment opportunities in rural areas, and to increase the output of home-grown food.[32]

These ex-servicemen taking up the offer of land after the war had quite an effect on the Lancashire landscape. A report of 1919 commented, "Poultry-keeping is carried on very extensively throughout the county, and forms a special industry in Preesall, Pilling, Stalmine, Hambleton, Great Eccleston, St Michaels, Woodplumpton, Barton and Garstang."[33] In an undated cutting from the *Westmorland Gazette*, Pilling-born agricultural journalist Jeff Swift remembered the hen cabins dotted over the fields. The new farmers were targeted by the LUPS taking their lectures around the county, and in booklets and chapters in books: W. Powell Owen dedicated a final chapter of his *Poultry-Keeping on Money-Making Lines* to "Poultry Farming as a Profession (with Special Reference to Ex-servicemen)."[34]

Pilling was once world famous for its poultry

Over the Gate

By Jeff Swift

IN THE late twenties and early thirties, the areas most heavily populated with poultry in the world were Pilling, in North Lancashire, and a parish in Japan, the name of which I can neither pronounce nor spell.

Most of the pasture fields in Pilling were dotted with hen cabins made of timber with a felted roof and the usual size was 24ft by 12ft. Inside the cabins were perches, droppings boards and nest boxes. The number of laying birds per cabin was regulated by how many hens could comfortably perch. The number varied according to the breed, the most popular at that time being what were known as "Rhody Blacks". They were a cross between Rhode Island Red and Black Leghorn; a heavy cross light breed. The resultant progeny were black in colour, of medium size and, of course, had the hybrid vigour.

Unless you could carry sufficient feed on your back, the favourite mode of transport was a pony and cart, the use of which meant you could also carry the required churns of water.

The feed consisted of whole oats scattered on the ground, pelleted feed, either scattered or fed in troughs, and sometimes meal.

Poultry, of course, don't like wet weather and during a wet time there was a lot of mud about and they could often look very bedraggled.

One reason you saw so many fields of laying hens was that a lot of servicemen, returning after the first World War and finding jobs difficult to get, spent their gratuities setting themselves up in business as smallholders or poultry farmers and continued to make a reasonable living until the eternal quest for cheap food meant they had to keep bigger and bigger numbers of birds and, in the end, most of them went out of business.

The moral of the story is: if people would like free range eggs, they can have them, so long as they are prepared to pay the extra costs of production; unless of course someone has the secret of producing free range eggs which do not incur extra costs, then please let me know and I'll pass on the good news.

I can remember one particular ex-soldier who was a great character and made his living out of a field of poultry. He was always cheerful and he used to say to us "Now lads, you've all been to school since I have, how can you buy eggs at a shilling a dozen, sell them at a shilling a dozen and still make a profit? And of course we didn't know, so we said: "We don't know Bill, how can you?"

"Easy," he would say, "You buy 'em at the Co-op and get divi!".

Fig. 2.5 Westmorland Gazette article

Between the Wars

There was some dispute as to the proportion of the country's hens contained within Lancashire. In a talk to the Preston and District Utility Poultry Society in 1923, the poultry instructor to the Lancashire County Council, Mr Dobbin, claimed there were more than 6,000,000 hens in Lancashire, and that it was by far the most important poultry county in the country.[35] A Mr S. L. Bennison visited Lancashire while surveying the nation's agriculture and disputed the official figure that Lancashire had a sixth of the nation's chickens, arguing it was nearer a third as holdings of less than an acre were not included in the official statistics.[36] A Ministry of Agriculture and Fisheries report of 1924 thought the county had 10% of the country's stock.[37]

The national attempts to organise poultry producers acknowledged the importance of Lancashire. In 1920 Preston was chosen as the venue for the first full meeting of the "National Poultry Parliament," later the National Poultry Council, which took place at County Hall.[38] Involved in the Parliament were representatives from national clubs and societies, agricultural colleges, and county council advisors. The concerns the Parliament outlined were over the number of foreign imports of eggs; the "distribution scheme," which was an attempt to improve stock by distributing eggs for hatching and day-old chicks at virtually cost price through 165 centres; and the establishment of a central poultry institute to disseminate good practice. The first president was Edward Brown, and the vice-president Mr Tom Barron,[39] both Lancashire men. The Parliament continued to meet annually up until the 1940s.[40]

Marketing Produce

The importance of marketing has been mentioned earlier, and it is something Lancashire farmers were among the first to address. The old methods of distribution had four alternatives: farmers sold directly to

The Mid-Lancashire Poultry Industry

Fig. 2.6 Sir Edward Brown and delegates at the 1934 conference. The names J. Collinson and Tom Barron appear regularly in poultry matters.

the consumer; to a retailer such as a local shopkeeper or a store in a nearby town; they sent their eggs to a market; they sold to a higgler, country dealer, or packing station. Sending eggs to auction was for the most part quite rare in Lancashire and was confined mostly to areas south of the Wash and east of Devon.[41] Up until the 1920s the higgler was the most important outlet, and in remote areas he was often also a general merchant who performed other services for the families on his round. When the higgler or other dealer had a glut of eggs and needed to move them on, as often happened in spring, then packing or transit stations came into being as a means of facilitating that movement, the first ones being noted around 1910.[42] The higgler set the prices, which were not always the best for the farmer, but after the Great War Lancashire farmers combined and by the 1920s egg prices in mid-

Lancashire were not determined by supply and demand, but were set on the recommendation of a small group of producers: in Garstang Jonathan Collinson and Jack Rigby, and in Preston Tom Barron, Jack Wrennall and Harry Sutton, and because of the influence of those two markets, prices throughout Lancashire were affected. Tom Barron was convinced that since that method of pricing had been introduced all the county's producers had benefited.[43]

This system was made more formal by the creation of the Lancashire Egg Producers' Society Ltd, with those same five on the board of directors, which collected the eggs from the farmer, tested and graded them, then packed them in clean boxes and forwarded them to the shopkeepers of the region. If a consumer requested it, the eggs would also be graded by colour.[44] The Society was pictured at work and held up as an exemplar in a Ministry Report on Marketing in 1927.[45]

FIG. 5.—Candling and grading home produce. The candling is carried out on the centre table on which the trays of eggs are placed above a strong light. Grading is done by hand. A lamp for single testing and scales for weighing doubtful eggs can be seen between the centre trays.
(*Reproduced by permission of the Lancashire Egg Producers, Ltd.*)

Fig. 2.7 Lancashire Egg Eackers at work. "Candling" was shining a light on the eggs to check for internal imperfections.

Jack Wrennall asserted that he and his fellow directors took no profits from the company, and Mr Wrennall estimated that by their efforts prices on Preston market had increased by at least 2d. per dozen.[46] The Society also used the telephone to contact the markets of Lancashire's major towns besides Preston and Garstang, ascertained where the best prices were to be had, and sent their eggs there.[47] That situation continued at least until 1933, when the LUPS awarded those men a testimonial in appreciation of their efforts, though understandably other groups of businessmen were also aware of the benefits of concerted action. LUPS felt they had to resist, for instance, overtures from the Preston Grocers' Association affiliated Preston and Fylde District Associated Egg Collectors to participate in price-setting discussions.[48]

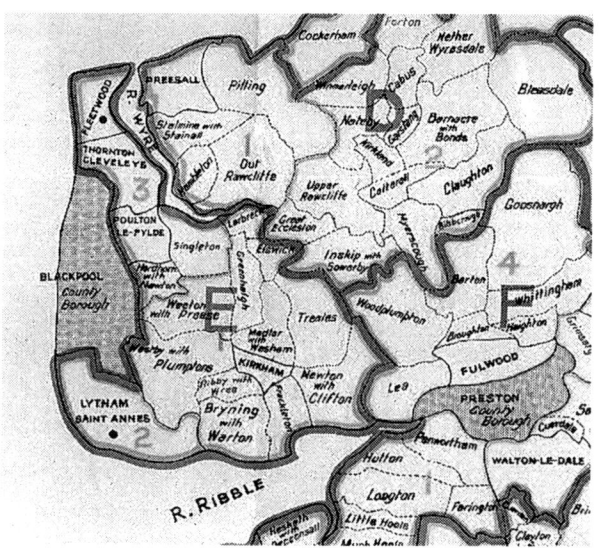

Fig. 2.8 Central Lancashire 1937. The two major markets of the region were Garstang and Preston. Egg prices were controlled by five major farmers.

Marketing Developments

Lancashire Egg Producers eventually merged with the larger Preston and District Farmers' Trading Society, which dealt in other products and also made animal feed. An undated speech, "a little chat," by Mr Whiteley, the manager and secretary of Preston Farmers, to an assemblage of poultry farmers, chronologically situated in the Preston Farmer records just after the merger discussions with Lancashire Egg Producers, explained the centrality of egg production to its trading and to the area. Preston Farmers was the largest agricultural trading society in the country; the largest "operator" of new-laid eggs in England; 60% of trade in feed was with poultry farmers; one third of all England's eggs were produced in a small area around Preston and production was increasing; the average price to the producer was higher in this part of the country than anywhere else. He finally exhorted farmers and Association to work together for mutual benefit, but asked the farmers to be more careful in the eggs they sent and weed out the broken eggs, the rotten eggs, the stale eggs, the dirty eggs and the stained eggs, and to avoid short supplies.[49] It was quite a piece of rhetoric, and though Lancashire was better at marketing its eggs than other areas, it acknowledged that standards could not be allowed to slip.

Lancashire Supreme

By the 1930s, Lancashire poultry farming was a big industry. A type of hen cabin common to the county was even known nationally as the "Lancashire Cabin." It usually measured 24 feet by 12 feet – "twenty-four-bi-twelve" was the commonly understood term for the whole cabin among Lancashire farmers. It had a slightly raised ridge on a corrugated iron roof to allow for ventilation; sliding glass windows along the sides, one foot from the floor; a further row of ventilator windows above that, known as "Lancashire Lights," which dropped backwards at the top a short distance into the cabin.[50]

Fig. 2.9 1933 LUPS testimonial to five stalwarts of the industry

The industry was of national, even international importance; stock was in demand all over the world. Though the presence of the industrial areas of mid and south Lancashire had provided a stimulus through their ready-made market for eggs, the 1930s road and rail facilities made the existence of a local market less important, and anyway there were plenty of potential customers through retail shops and private buyers and at country markets.[51]

The producers were not short of more imaginative ideas for transporting their stock. Hamnett's of Blackpool even took advantage of

Fig. 2.10 Cut-away Lancashire brooder cabin. This is a scaled-down display model from the works of Jack Wrennall.

Fig. 2.11 Poultry Market, Lune Street 1939 (Preston Digital Archive)

Fig. 2.12 Day-old chicks being despatched to Romania from Blackpool Airport, 1936.

Fig. 2.13 Insulated box for transporting eggs for incubation

the local airport. They used the transport infrastructure even for the most fragile materials, and special packaging was designed. The box in Figure 2.13 is for transporting eggs for the buyer to incubate.

Alan Howkins notes that by 1939 poultry farming nationally had moved well beyond the housewife's "pin money" or "hen money" and accounted for £29 million per annum, more than the non-subsidised value of grain crops. He also observes that the area around Preston "supported a huge and well-organised poultry industry."[52] Howkins points out another feature of Lancashire farmers – the willingness to work together for the good of all – which he exemplifies with the Preston and District Farmers Trading Society, "founded in 1911 to buy poultry feed collectively for small and medium producers."[53] The Lancashire Utility Poultry Society is another such example.

Notes

1   Sir Edward Brown, *British Poultry Husbandry: Its Evolution and History* (London: Chapman and Hall's, 1930), p. 258.

2   L. Frank Baum, *The Book of the Hamburgs: A Brief Treatise upon the Mating, Rearing and Management of the Different Varieties of Hamburgs* (Hartford, Connecticut. H. H. Stoddard, 1886), p. 13.

3   Royal Commission on Agriculture. Mr Coleman's Reports to the Royal Commission on Agriculture on Northumberland, Lancashire and Cheshire, House of Commons Parliamentary Papers 1882.

4   Brown, *British Poultry Husbandry*, p. 255.

5   Brown, *British Poultry Husbandry*, p. 259.

6   Brown, *British Poultry Husbandry*, pp. 76–7.

7   Brown, *British Poultry Husbandry*, p. 256.

8   "Poultry at the 'Royal' Show," *Preston Guardian*, 26 July 1884; Issue 3732.

9   H. Easom Smith, *Modern Poultry Development* (Liss, Hampshire. Spur Publications, 1976), p. 26.

10   Easom Smith, *Modern Poultry Development*, pp. 29–30.

11   Brown, *British Poultry Husbandry*, p. 255.
12   "The Official Agricultural Returns," *Preston Guardian*, 8 November 1884, p. 4.
13   Ministry of Agriculture and Fisheries, *Eggs and Poultry: Report of the Reorganisation Commission for Great Britain* (London. HMSO, 1935), p. 16.
14   Christabel S. Orwin and Edith H. Whetham, *History of British Agriculture: 1846–1914* (Newton Abbot. David and Charles, 1971), p. 184.
15   T. W. Fletcher, "Lancashire Livestock Farming during the Great Depression," in P. J. Perry, *British Agriculture 1875–1914* (London. Methuen and Co., 1973), p. 80.
16   Michael Winstanley, "Industrialization and the Small Farm: Family and Household Economy in Nineteenth-Century Lancashire," *Past & Present*, No. 152 (Aug. 1996), p. 157.
17   Orwin and Whetham, *History of British Agriculture: 1846–1914*, p. 184.
18   Fletcher, "Lancashire Livestock Farming during the Great Depression," in Perry, *British Agriculture 1875–1914*, p. 80.
19   Fletcher, "Lancashire Livestock Farming during the Great Depression," in Perry, *British Agriculture 1875–1914*, p. 82. Fletcher uses two early twentieth-century works, G. H. Wood, *The History of the Cotton Trade during the Past Hundred Years* (1910), p. 128, and W. T. Layton, *An Introduction to the Study of Prices* (1912), p. 150.
20   Fletcher, "Lancashire Livestock Farming during the Great Depression," p. 82.
21   Winstanley, "Industrialization and the Small Farm," p. 173.
22   Fletcher, "Lancashire Livestock Farming during the Great Depression," p. 83.
23   Royal Commission on Agriculture. Reports by Mr Wilson-Fox on the Garstang District of Lancashire and the Glendale District of Northumberland, House of Commons Parliamentary Papers 1894, p. 7.
24   Royal Commission on Agriculture. Reports by Mr Wilson-Fox on the Garstang District of Lancashire and the Glendale District of Northumberland, House of Commons Parliamentary Papers 1894, p. 63.
25   "In a Pilling Orchard: Fruit Culture at Sandside Farm," *Preston Guardian*, 26 May 1928, p. 11.
26   Royal Commission on Agriculture. Reports by Mr Wilson-Fox on the Garstang District of Lancashire and the Glendale District of Northumberland, House of Commons Parliamentary Papers 1894, p. 62.
27   Edith H. Whetham, *The Agrarian History of England and Wales, Vol. VIII: 1914–1939* (Cambridge. Cambridge University Press, 1978), p. 122.
28   Whetham, *Agrarian History of England and Wales, Vol. VIII*, p. 128.

29 Sir Edward Brown, *Memories at Eventide* (Burnley, Lancashire. John Dixon, 1934), p. 220.
30 "Land for Ex-soldiers," *Preston Guardian*, 1 February 1919, p. 5.
31 "Small Holdings in Lancashire," *Preston Guardian*, 14 March 1925, p. 9.
32 Whetham, *Agrarian History of England and Wales, Vol. VIII*, pp. 137–8.
33 Board of Agriculture and Fisheries, *Wages and Conditions of Employment in Agriculture, Vol. II: Reports* (1919), p. 138.
34 W. Powell-Owen, *Poultry-Keeping on Money-Making Lines* (London. George Newnes, 1919), pp. 253–6.
35 "6,000,000 Hens: Lancashire's Huge Stock of Poultry," *Preston Guardian*, 3 May 1924, p. 15.
36 "Poultry Industry: Impressions of Lancashire's Enterprise," *Preston Guardian*, 16 July 1927, p. 7.
37 Ministry of Agriculture and Fisheries, *Report on Egg Marketing in England and Wales* (London. HMSO, 1927), p. 2.
38 "Poultry Parliament: National Assembly at Preston," *Preston Guardian*, 17 July 1920, p. 6.
39 Brown, *Memories at Eventide*, p. 225.
40 "Poultry Parliament: National Assembly at Preston," p. 6.
41 Ministry of Agriculture and Fisheries, *Eggs and Poultry: Report of the Reorganisation Commission for Great Britain* (London. HMSO, 1935), p. 19.
42 Ministry of Agriculture and Fisheries, *Eggs and Poultry*, p. 21.
43 "Egg Markets: Problems of Stabilising Prices," *Preston Guardian*, 7 February 1925, p. 13.
44 Ministry of Agriculture and Fisheries, *Eggs and Poultry*, p. 40.
45 Ministry of Agriculture and Fisheries, *Report on Egg Marketing in England and Wales*, pp. 33, 36–7.
46 "Egg Markets: Problems of Stabilising Prices," p. 13.
47 "Poultry Industry: Impressions of Lancashire's Enterprise," p. 7.
48 "Egg Prices at Garstang and Preston," *Preston Guardian*, 8 October 1927, p. 10.
49 MERL CR PFL AD1/2. Undated talk by Mr Whiteley to poultry farmers, Preston Farmers' Minutes, 1922 onwards.
50 William W. Broomhead, *Poultry Breeding and Management* (London. New Era Publishing Co. [1937]), pp. 46–7.
51 Broomhead, *Poultry Breeding and Management*, p. 384.

52 Alan Howkins, *The Death of Rural England: A Social History of the Countryside since 1900* (London and New York: Routledge, 2004), p. 72.
53 Howkins, *Death of Rural England*, p. 72.

3

THE LANCASHIRE UTILITY POULTRY SOCIETY

The Lancashire Utility Poultry Society (LUPS) was formed at a meeting in the Reform Club, Chapel Street, Preston, on 10 January 1918. Initially the aim was "to advance the interests of the breed, to devise means for easing the food difficulties during the war, and to prepare for development on the declaration of peace, when, it is believed, the industry will undergo enormous expansion."[1] In the same year they produced their first yearbook, and this and future yearbooks gave the aims more expansively under a "Rules" section as "to encourage the breeding of pure breeds and first crosses for Utility purposes," and the methods of encouragement to be used included exhibitions, lectures, essays, practical demonstrations and laying competitions.[2]

The Committee, and First Meetings

At the first meeting, Tom Barron of Catforth was appointed chairman, and he made the point that poultry keeping had long been regarded as a side-line of farming, and that one of the Society's aims should be to raise its status. Membership was fixed at 5 shillings. Mr Dobbin of the Lancashire County Council Farm at Hutton attended, as did members of other societies such as Mr Longbottom of the Northern Utility Poultry Society. Jonathan Collinson of Lingart Farm, Barnacre, Garstang, became a committee member.[3] The full committee was elected at the subsequent Annual General Meeting of Thursday 24 January.[4]

Evidence of the reach of the Society is found in the programme of events for its third year of existence, which included meetings around central Lancashire, in Preston, Freckleton, Catforth and Chorley. Meetings were well attended and remembered as being social, entertaining events.[5] Topics included "Selection and Breeding," "Diseases of Poultry" and "Mendelism: Its Application to Poultry Breeding." Two asides might be permitted here. Speakers tended to be ordinary practising members like Jack Wrennall and Tom Barron, though speaker "W. Thompson B.Sc." was proud to display his scientific credentials as well.[6] He must have been inordinately proud of his degree, as whenever the poultry farmers of Lancashire appeared in a group photograph the "BSc" was always appended after his name, and even in the list of those attending Jack Wrennall's funeral in 1944 he remained "W. Thompson B.S.C."[7] "Mendelism" seemed to hold a particular interest for poultry breeders, and several articles appeared in books and journals around this time linking the work of Gregor Mendel on heredity and variation to poultry, often accompanied by complicated diagrams and equations.[8]

Evolution

At the Annual General Meeting of September 1920, Tom Barron announced that he felt it was best if he gave up being president after one more year as he felt that "change of leaders was good for any organisation."[9] He was not a man to accept situations without question and appreciated the need for new blood and fresh approaches, and also he himself was busy in other areas. The main thrust of that meeting was to push forward three objectives: the abolition of price controls which would make egg production cheaper; the marking of foreign eggs with the name of the country of origin or the port through which they entered the country; and the need for local egg-collecting depots controlled by the farmers themselves.[10]

LUPS continued to encourage its members to look forward, and in hindsight the advice given was eminently sensible. Edward Brown, president of the International Poultry Association and later "Sir" Edward Brown, was a regular speaker. At a meeting in Preston on Wednesday 11 November 1925 attended by poultry farmers from all over the north of England, Brown gave his views on the new developments in the poultry world, in particular what he had seen in a recent visit to Canada and the USA. Distance from the markets had meant that North American farmers had to organise collectively, and his other observations and suggestions were equally pertinent: breeders and producers needed to work closely together, small farmers ("ten hen men") were important in increasing overall egg production and reducing imports, equipment run on electricity was going to be important and farms should gain access to it as quickly as possible, and the "British poultry industry spent all too little" on advertising.[11]

LUPS Campaigns

From its early days LUPS was a campaigning body. The marking of foreign eggs became a particular hobbyhorse. In December 1926 LUPS invited Sydney Smith, Minister of Agriculture for Northern Ireland, to speak to them on the subject of marketing eggs, complimenting him in the vote of thanks with what is in hindsight a rather unfortunate epithet: the "Mussolini of the egg trade." The Society then pressured him to lobby the Government to grade all eggs, to market the benefits of new-laid eggs and to mark all eggs that had been kept in cold storage – all of which would discourage the public from buying imported eggs and assure them of the quality of the home-grown product.[12] Tom Barron was still working to persuade a government standing committee to mark imported eggs in 1928.[13] There was a great deal of opposition to the agitation, even from the great Sir Edward Brown who believed you should never advertise your trade opponents.[14] That particular battle was finally won in 1929, when the Government passed an Act that all imported eggs should be marked with the country of origin, and in his address to the members of LUPS Tom Barron celebrated that victory: "1929 will be remembered as a red-letter year by all poultry keepers."[15]

Despite Mr Barron's triumphalism, the actual effects were not clear cut. The immediate effect was only a slight reduction in the number of imported eggs; a report of 1935 expressed the belief that the reduction was mostly due to severe weather on the continent,[16] and the competition from imported eggs remained an issue. The president of the LUPS in 1931, Mr W. Gardner, claimed that Britain imported £20 million in eggs and poultry meat, including £2 million of tinned liquid eggs, mostly from China – "liquid filth" as he termed it. His appeal was not for protection from imports, but that the poultry industry should make itself so efficient that it could compete favourably with foreign opposition.[17] The home share of the market did increase, though, as the table shows.

Origins of domestic egg consumption 1924–33[18]

	Million Eggs		
	1924	1930	1933
Home Produced	2590 (52%)	3885 (52%)	4727 (68%)
Foreign Supplies	1777 (35.5%)	2474 (36%)	1475 (20.5%)
Dominion Supplies	624 (12.5%)	698 (12%)	727 (11.5%)
Total	4991	7057	6929

Publicity

The Society was also a good publicist: details of meetings were passed on to the local newspapers, and awards evenings were given ample coverage.

Fig. 3.1 1934 presentation evening. An impressive array of trophies.

LUPS Yearbooks

The contents of the yearbooks indicate the Society's other concerns. Results of laying trials are recorded comprehensively, and there are quite scientific articles on breeding, on combatting illnesses, and on the best nutrients. There are lists of practical cost considerations, with tables of weekly egg prices in Garstang and Preston over the previous two years, and charts to indicate the charges for sending goods by train. There is also a comprehensive register of the Society's officials and members; by the 1939 yearbook 1,174 members' names and addresses are listed.[19] Several essays discuss the relative merits of the various methods of farming employed in Lancashire; other articles analyse foodstuffs, the hen's metabolism and the constituent parts of eggs incredibly closely, referencing the scientific resources deployed by government researchers. E. T. Halman gave his research in detail in 1930: "From the figures I obtained I found that 200 2 oz. eggs contain 44 oz. protein, 34 oz. fat, 18 oz. lime, 2 oz. phosphorous pentoxide, $^4/_5$ oz. sulphur, $^2/_3$ oz. potassium oxide, 1 oz. sodium oxide and $^1/_2$ oz. chlorine."[20] His conclusion was that birds would not lay well on cereals alone, they needed supplements of protein, lime and sodium, and he advised his readers on which foods would provide them.[21]

Working Together

What the Society epitomised was the willingness of Lancashire poultry farmers to work together to advance their industry. They did not shrug their shoulders and accept situations which they perceived as unfair, in particular the competition from foreign eggs, but lobbied for change. Another campaign was against a taxation anomaly which operated against those who farmed poultry alone in that they, unlike farmers of cattle, sheep and other forms of animal husbandry, did not qualify for a lower rate of taxation. LUPS took two test cases to court at Preston and in each case the Commissioners decided in favour of the poultry farmers, though the Inland Revenue did not concede and prosecuted a poultry farmer named "Cook" in the High Court, a case which was heard in June 1923. Tom Barron took the issue to the National Poultry Parliament which was meeting that month in Blackpool; he asked for a fund to be instigated to help fight the case, and typically he started the fund with a personal donation of £25.[22] The battle continued until in 1926 LUPS supported William Nuttall of Longridge in contending that he should be assessed for tax purposes within schedule B rather than schedule D in a case which was heard in the King's Bench Division in London. Mr Justice Rowlett came down in favour of Mr Nuttall,[23] and lobbying continued until legislation in 1928 finally signalled a victory for the poultry farmers.[24] By combining, they were also able to protect themselves in other ways: at a meeting in Hoole in 1926, Mr Collier, the Society's secretary, explained the benefits of the Society's recently introduced insurance scheme by which eggs, incubators and brooders could be insured relatively cheaply against loss.[25]

Farming Know-how

A Ministry of Agriculture and Fisheries report was clear on the reasons behind Lancashire's predominance in poultry farming – it was the expertise of the farmers themselves. "The intensive production of Lancashire … can be traced, in part, to the location in the county of noted breeders of high fecund stock."[26] The Lancashire Utility Poultry Society showed clearly what those Lancashire poultry farmers could do when they banded together. They disseminated knowledge, taking their expertise to relatively remote areas where poultry farmers might otherwise feel quite isolated; they organised marketing strategies and worked together to achieve the best prices; they protected their members. The leaders of the Society were active farmers, and three of them in particular came to the forefront in mid-Lancashire, given authority nationally by their status as successful farmers: Jonathan Collinson, Jack Wrennall and Tom Barron. Their names have appeared frequently already, and their careers will now be briefly investigated.

Notes

1 "Future of Utility Poultry," *Preston Guardian*, 5 January 1918, p. 7.
2 The Lancashire Utility Poultry Society, "Rules"; printed in each yearbook.
3 "Formation of Utility Poultry Society," *Preston Guardian*, 12 January 1918, p. 3.
4 *Preston Guardian*, 26 January 1918, p. 5.
5 Thomas E. Whittle, *A Triumph of Science: A 70 Year History of the U.K. Poultry Industry* (self-published [1997]), p. 10.
6 "The Lancashire Utility Poultry Society," *Preston Guardian*, 6 December 1919, p. 8.
7 "Funeral of Mr John Wrennall: Many Tributes," *Preston Guardian*, 1 April 1944, p. 7.

8   Rev. E. Lewis Jones, "Mendelism and Its Application to Poultry Breeding," in S. H. Lewer, *Wright's Book of Poultry: Revised and Edited in Accordance with the Latest Poultry Club Standards* (London. Cassell and Co., 1913), pp. 5–14. "(R + R) (D + R) = 2RR + 2DR," p. 11.

9   "Utility Poultry: Lancashire Society's Meeting at Preston," *Preston Guardian*, 18 September 1920, p. 8.

10   "Utility Poultry: Lancashire Society's Meeting at Preston," p. 8.

11   "Poultry Topics: Mr E. Brown's Lecture at Preston," *Preston Guardian*, 14 November 1925, p. 7.

12   "Marketing of Eggs: Lancashire Poultry Keepers Urge Compulsory Grading," *Preston Guardian*, 18 December 1926, p. 15.

13   "Imported Eggs: M.P.s Objections to Marking Order," *The Times*, 18 April 1928, p. 5.

14   Sir Edward Brown, *Memories at Eventide* (Burnley, Lancashire. John Dixon, 1934), p. 109.

15   Tom Barron, "To the Members of the Lancashire Utility Poultry Society," Lancashire Utility Poultry Society Yearbook, 1930, p. 5.

16   Ministry of Agriculture and Fisheries, *Eggs and Poultry: Report of the Reorganisation Commission for Great Britain* (London. HMSO, 1935), p. 16.

17   Mr W. Gardner, "To the Members of the Lancashire Utility Poultry Society," Lancashire Utility Poultry Society Yearbook, 1931 (Preston. LUPS. R. Seed, printer), p. 4.

18   Ministry of Agriculture and Fisheries, *Eggs and Poultry*, p. 10.

19   "List of Members," Lancashire Utility Poultry Society Yearbook, 1939, pp. 79–111.

20   E. T. Halman, "Feeding for Egg Production," Lancashire Utility Poultry Society Yearbook, 1930, p. 9.

21   Halman, "Feeding for Egg Production," p. 11.

22   "National Poultry Parliament: Meetings at Blackpool," *Preston Guardian*, 30 June 1923, p. 11.

23   "Poultry Appeal: Longridge Case in the King's Bench," *Preston Guardian*, 13 March 1926, p. 4.

24   Brown, *Memories at Eventide*, pp. 228–9.

25   "Chicken Rearing: Hints on Incubator Management," *Preston Guardian*, 6 February 1926, p. 11.

26   Ministry of Agriculture and Fisheries, *Report on Egg Marketing in England and Wales* (London. HMSO, 1927), p. 2.

4

COLLINSON'S OF GARSTANG

Jonathan Collinson was born in 1885 in Catterall near Garstang into a farming family. His parents had farmed Woodacre Hall Farm in Garstang.[1] An invoice dated 7 October 1910 from "Thomas Barron" shows that Mr Collinson was farming at Salisbury's, Nether Wyresdale, Scorton: the invoice was for "8 Best White Dotte hens, 1909 progeny 5/- each" and "2 Best White Leghorn Cockerels 15/- each."[2] Perhaps the first birds of the Collinson Empire? Mr Collinson's major farming association was with Higher Lingart Farm, Barnacre, which is where he was living by the 1911 census, though that return classes him as a "dairy farmer," with no mention of poultry.[3] He maintained his dairy interest and up until 1952 he was a member of the "British Friesian Club."[4] Though his address eventually became the "Lingart Poultry Farm," his catalogue of 1933 showed that he was not entirely dependent upon poultry. The 90-acre farm had 30 dairy cows, 70 breeding ewes, a herd of 50 to 60 pigs and 10 acres of arable land, besides the 10,000 laying hens.[5] His annual return to the Ministry of Agriculture for that same year shows a couple of discrepancies – 42 pigs, and 8,000 laying hens – and also states he employed 10 males of 21 years and over, 4 males under 21, and 2 women and girls.[6]

Laying Tests

Mr Collinson was early in his farming career aware of the value of laying tests in improving the strains of poultry, and their value in publicity. He won local competitions, but also followed Tom Barron's lead and took part in international competitions, and indeed, won prizes, though entered fewer competitions into the 1920s.

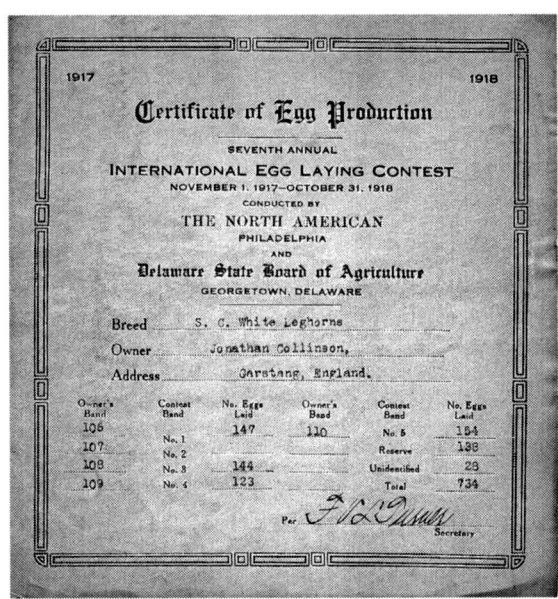

Fig. 4.1 Delaware State Board of Agriculture Certificate, 1918

He was a little less conspicuous in poultry county or national affairs than Tom Barron and Jack Wrennall. Neither did he involve himself in village politics; at least his name did not appear in the newspapers as doing so, though he was a church warden and a member of the Parochial Church Council.[7] Though he did lecture occasionally he tended not to judge at shows. He was, however, a server on committees: LUPS, the Lancashire Federation of Poultry Societies, and the National Poultry Congress,[8] so one can assume he was held in some regard by his peers.

Brooders

As with the other professional breeders, Mr Collinson was an early advocate of the hover brooder which meant he could rear chickens in far greater numbers than by having the chickens reared naturally by the mother: in a lecture to Pilling poultry farmers in 1919 he said he had been using such paraffin brooders for three years,[9] and an undated early catalogue, before his catalogues had his "Poultry for Profit" slogan on the front, claimed "Mr Collinson was the first man in Lancashire to rear chicks with Brooder stoves."[10] By 1920 he was advertising a coal-fired brooder of his own invention.[11] It was a rather strange contraption which he claimed could also be used to heat a house or shed, but the design was actually both practical and ingenious. The brooder is created by the stove having a cowl or hood fitted, as the picture from his advertisement shows (see Figure 4.3):

Business Sense

Jonathan Collinson was keen to stress the scientific side of his business. He told W. Powell Owen he had 200 trap nests in daily use, and Mr Powell Owen pronounced, "There is no more scientific breeder of high-class utility stock than Mr Collinson."[12] He also seems to have been quite marketing aware and was producing a catalogue at least from the early 1920s, a catalogue which tried to personalise both his farm and his family members yet provide easily read information on his products, so the overall impression is of both friendliness and efficiency. The example in Figure 4.4 is from 1933 where he describes his family's roles in the business.

Fig. 4.2 The Collinson coal-fired brooder

Fig. 4.3 The coal-fired brooder fully erected

Another example of his awareness of the value of publicity in poultry circles is his desire to have his farm featured in the magazines of the time, and among his papers is a letter from *Poultry* magazine dated 21 September 1920 thanking him for four photographs he had sent to accompany a review of his farm which was appearing in their magazine.[13] In June 1923 he hosted the delegates of the National Poultry Parliament

Fig. 4.4 The Collinson family business structure

at his farm, which was there described as "one of the largest in the north," with 10,000 laying birds, 20,000 young stock on 40 acres of his property. A special feature was the sunken incubator house which could deal with 20,000 eggs at once and hatched annually between 60,000 to 80,000 chickens. His egg-packing station was responsible for packing and despatching 6,000 eggs daily to Lancashire's towns and markets.[14]

Mr Collinson again appeared in a poultry-related publication when his farm was featured in *The Feathered World*'s Fourth World Poultry

Congress Supplement in 1930. The article is as much advertisement as description, and stresses a logical, scientific approach: laying and stock records were kept, potential breeders trap-nested and blood-tested. The incubators had a capacity of 40,000 eggs, but incubation ceased after May

Fig. 4.5 "Gloucester" incubators on the Collinson farm

each year; when not used for incubation the room was not wasted, it was used as a cheese store. Mrs Collinson was the daughter of Joseph Gornall, a legendary Lancashire cheese producer and inventor of the Gornall Patent Cheesemaker, patented in 1892 and widely used in the area.[15] Understandably, the dairy was her responsibility. Sheep and chickens grazed together. Her husband remained faithful to his anthracite brooder stoves, and no mention is made of any future conversion to electricity, possibly because his farm was rather more remote than Tom Barron's which was about to be converted at that time. He was experimenting with battery brooders, "for we must give things a trial," but did not seem keen. Interestingly, cockerels were not identified and culled from the start, but allowed to grow with the others for a few weeks and then killed and sold as *petites poussins* at 1 to 1½ lb. As was the case seven years before, egg production was important to the economy of the farm. Four thousand laying pullets and hens were divided into flocks of 200, and half the total laying stock was replaced every year, so no bird was over two and a half years old. Eggs were still packed on the farm and distributed locally. Besides the sheep, cattle and horses also grazed among the laying hens. The hens fed off the farm's own mash, made on site "in an oil-driven mixing machine."

A member of his staff was dedicated to clerical work, including maintaining a register which recorded the performances of the breeding birds, blood-testing results and egg weights. No chick was bred from a bird which did not lay a 2 oz egg. The article claims a bird's pedigree could be traced back 13 years.[16]

Agricultural Shows

Mr Collinson was also a regular attender at the prestigious Royal Lancashire Agricultural Show – specific details of the Show held in Liverpool in August 1923 are among his papers: he was entering the "Implements and Machinery" section.[17] An undated picture from his records shows his stand at one of the shows, and also confirms his liking for a slogan: "Experientia Docet" was on early catalogues, later replaced by "Poultry for Profit" and here he advises "Go With the Times" (see Figure 4.6).

Diversification

Jonathan Collinson was in many ways successful because he embraced diversity. Though his farm was a "poultry farm" in its title, he was not just dependent upon hens, but realised that as poultry keeping burgeoned in popularity there was also profit to be made from poultry-related products:

Fig. 4.6 The Collinson stall at an agricultural show

brooders, feeders and feeds. The Collinsons developed and marketed three different-sized dry mash feeders, the "Lingart Dry Mash Hopper," "the outcome of years of experience and practice," as his advertising leaflet of 1922 says.[18]

He also provided the feed that went into the feeders. His first mill was not at the farm, which was to the east of Garstang and relatively remote, but in the town itself on Church Street, accessible by road, rail and canal. His speciality was producing ready-made dry mash feedstuff for farmers. An article of 1924 announcing that he would be vice-chairman of the general committee of the LUPS refers to him as the "pioneer of dry mash feeding."[19] Wet mash, as noted by an American observer of Lancashire Poultry farming, Dr B. F. Kaupp, was used more in Britain than in America and tended to make the hens eat more.[20] It was felt to be easily digestible and therefore was often fed as the first meal of the day to give the birds a good start.[21] The wet mash/dry mash issue caused so much debate among

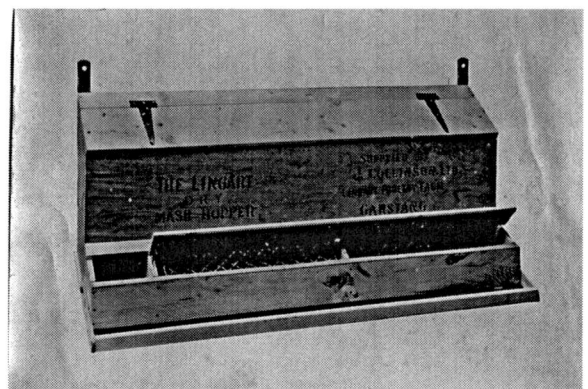

Fig. 4.7 Lingart dry mash hopper

Fig. 4.8 Collinsons' Mill, Church Street, Garstang, 1920s

Lancashire's poultry farmers that LUPS arranged a trial between the two methods and a third involving a mixture of wet mash in the morning and dry mash at night. Over two years' experimentation, wet mash alone and dry mash alone produced similar results, while the most productive was the mixture,[22] but each method had its own adherents who would not by convinced by the claims of others. Collinson advertising claimed that dry mash made feeding simpler as there was less preparation involved, and also the birds made their own saliva which enabled them to digest the food properly and so gain more nutrients.[23] Whether true or not, his argument seems to have a scientific basis and so carries weight.

An early catalogue of his products shows he sold Black Leghorns, White Wyandottes, White Leghorns and Buff Orpingtons.[24] A later catalogue of 1938 lists Rhode Island Reds, Black Leghorns, and crosses of those two breeds, as well as the White Wyandottes and White Leghorns.[25] He had discarded the more ornamental Buff Orpingtons and was concentrating

Fig. 4.9 Lancashire cabins on the Collinsons' farm – probably 1930s

on the accepted utility breeds in the industry, so he was offering a safe, conservative stock.

Not a Man to Mess With

Jonathan Collinson was prepared to agitate at the highest level over poultry issues. Among his papers there are copies of an exchange of letters between himself, his MP, H. Ramsbotham, and Walter Elliott, the Minister of Agriculture, throughout February 1935, concerning the number of imports of foreign eggs, a perennial issue. Mr Collinson is concerned with the depressed state of the poultry industry, the blame for which he lays directly at the door of foreign imports, and threatens electoral blackmail:

> *There is a growing feeling that if nothing is done then at the forthcoming election you will have a great rift from Conservatism, and the party who will promise to do something for the industry will most certainly get the votes.*[26]

The Minister's reply indicates that the Government was negotiating with foreign countries to reduce imports and had achieved qualified success, and, in the universal manner of governments faced with agitation, had formed a committee: "Your constituent will no doubt have noticed in the press that a Great Britain Reorganisation Commission for Eggs and Poultry has now been constituted."[27]

An early and increasingly acrimonious exchange of letters suggests that Mr Collinson could be firm, even ruthless, in his business dealings. In February 1917 he ordered a "T" type gas engine from the National Gas Engine Company of Ashton-Under-Lyne: their acknowledgement of the order is dated 5 February 1917, and there is no reference to any money changing hands. The cost was £284, "80% on delivery, and balance in one month."[28] A letter of 12 June indicates the company is progressing with the engine, and as it is their first transaction with Mr Collinson then they suggest he send a cheque for the full amount. A further letter of 7 July informs Mr Collinson the engine is nearly complete and asks for payment before the engine is despatched, and subsequent letters are sent demanding payment before delivery, including threats that the Government might requisition the engine and if Mr Collinson wants it he should pay immediately.[29] That threat was shown to be empty, as by 8 April 1918 it is apparent that Mr Collinson has looked elsewhere:

> *We understand from our Mr Cryer that you have purchased a secondhand gas engine, and consequently we must insist on your paying us an indemnity of 15% on the contract price as per enclosed invoice and unless we receive a cheque in settlement by return we shall have to place the matter in other hands for attention.*
>
> *Considering that we kept the engine which you ordered in our stock for many weeks, we think you have treated us very badly indeed; hence our action.*

They enclose a bill for £39 12s.[30] The resolution of the problem is not among the papers, but it seems unlikely from the tone of the correspondence that Mr Collinson capitulated, and that as the original agreement asked for cash on delivery he was within his legal rights to remain firm, though the business ethics of acquiring a second-hand machine after ordering a new one can perhaps be called into question.

Trouble at t'Mill

Of the three farms under discussion, though, the Collinson farm was not a story of unqualified success. It is apparent that during the autumn of 1925 the business was in trouble. Notice of voluntary liquidation appeared in the *London Gazette*,[31] and the local auctioneer, Edward Hothersall, contacted Mr Collinson enquiring whether there was to be a sale; but that same letter suggested that "Mr Brockholes," presumably Mr Fitzherbert-Brockholes, a landlord and a prominent, much respected figure in Lancashire agriculture, was on the side of the Collinsons and was going to his head office in Manchester to try to sort things out.[32] A list of creditors among his papers shows that 44 businesses were owed a total of £2,938 17s. 11d. to corn merchants, notably W. J. Pye (£381 0s. 6d.), who was owed the most. No mention of financial difficulties appeared in the local press. Mr Collinson continued in his duties as president of LUPS that year, and invoices and receipts continued to come in, and so presumably the storm was weathered. No further mention is made of the mill in Garstang, so it is possible those premises were sacrificed and that side of the business temporarily jettisoned and then relocated to the farm. Later catalogues still advertise his own feeds, though now produced "at my place, prepared and blended by the finest machinery, under my personal supervision."[33] The *Feathered World* visit already noted had described his mash as being made at the farm.

Mr Collinson died in 1953. He had been ill for some time, and while his passing was noticed in the *Preston Guardian*, he was not given the plaudits awarded to other poultry barons, possibly because his illness had occasioned a relatively long period of inactivity, but also possibly because while he publicised his products imaginatively and effectively, he was not such a self-publicist as some in entering or judging high-profile competitions, nor as at ease with the social trappings of being a leading poultryman.

Notes

1   The National Archive UK, 1901 Census, Lancashire, Garstang Parish, Barnacre with Bonds (District 1-02), p. 20.
2   Invoice from Thomas Barron to Jonathan Collinson, 7 October 1910. From the papers of Jonathan Collinson held by John Higginson of the Fylde Country Life Preservation Society.
3   The National Archive UK, 1911 Census, Lancashire, Garstang Parish, Barnacre with Bonds (District 1-02), Schedule 9.
4   Letter from L. R. Dunderdale, 20 January 1953, to J. Collinson and Sons regarding unpaid subscription to British Friesian Breeders' Club. From the papers of Jonathan

Collinson held by John Higginson of the Fylde Country Life Preservation Society.

5   "Poultry for Profit Catalogue 1933." From the papers of Jonathan Collinson held by John Higginson of the Fylde Country Life Preservation Society.

6   Ministry of Agriculture and Fisheries, Particulars as on 3 June 1933, J. Collinson, High Lingart. From the papers of Jonathan Collinson held by John Higginson of the Fylde Country Life Preservation Society.

7   "Funeral of Well-Known Garstang Poultryman," *Preston Guardian*, 7 March 1953, p. 4.

8   "Poultry Council," *Preston Guardian*, 22 January 1927, p. 7.

9   "Mr J. Collinson's Lecture at Pilling," *Preston Guardian*, 25 January 1919, p. 10.

10 Undated Collinson catalogue, p. 16. From the papers of Jonathan Collinson held by John Higginson of the Fylde Country Life Preservation Society.

11 "Jonathan Collinson Ltd." Undated catalogue, probably from the early 1920s. From the papers of Jonathan Collinson held by John Higginson of the Fylde Country Life Preservation Society.

12 W. Powell-Owen, *Poultry-Keeping on Money-Making Lines* (London. George Newnes, 1919), p. 199.

13 Letter from *Poultry* editor F. J. Broomhead, dated 21 September 1920, from the papers of Jonathan Collinson held by John Higginson of the Fylde Country Life Preservation Society.

14 "National Poultry Parliament: Meetings at Blackpool," *Preston Guardian*, 30 June 1923, p. 11.

15 http://www.lancashirepioneers.com/gornall/cheese.asp. 09/05/2012 It is a feature of the poultry and dairy industries in Lancashire that the farmers themselves came up with many designs for machinery.

16 "A Great Lancashire Poultry Farm," *The Feathered World*, 18 July 1930, pp. xiv–xvi.

17 Royal Agricultural Society to Mr Jonathan Collinson. Undated envelope and entry form. From the papers of Jonathan Collinson held by John Higginson of the Fylde Country Life Preservation Society.

18 "Lingart Dry Mash Hopper." From the papers of Jonathan Collinson held by John Higginson of the Fylde Country Life Preservation Society.

19 "Utility Poultry Experts: County Society's New Appointments," *Preston Guardian*, 4 October 1924.

20 "American Scientist's Visit to Lancashire," *Preston Guardian*, 20 August 1921, p. 2.

21 E. T. Brown, *The Poultry Keeper's Text Book* (London. Ward Lock and Co.,

1934), p. 117.

22 "Poultry Problems: Lancashire Society's Experiments," *Preston Guardian*, 22 August 1922, p. 12.

23 Undated Collinson Ltd advertising leaflet. From the papers of Jonathan Collinson held by John Higginson of the Fylde Country Life Preservation Society.

24 "Jonathan Collinson Ltd." Undated catalogue, probably from the early 1920s. From the papers of Jonathan Collinson held by John Higginson of the Fylde Country Life Preservation Society.

25 "Poultry for Profit: Mating List 1938. Jonathan Collinson, Lingart Poultry Farm, Garstang, Lancs." From the papers of Jonathan Collinson held by John Higginson of the Fylde Country Life Preservation Society.

26 Letter dated 4 February 1935 from Jonathan Collinson to Herwald Ramsbotham MP. From the papers of Jonathan Collinson held by John Higginson of the Fylde Country Life Preservation Society.

27 Letter dated 7 February 1935 from Walter Elliott to H. Ramsbotham. From the papers of Jonathan Collinson held by John Higginson of the Fylde Country Life Preservation Society.

28 The National Gas Engine Company to J. Collinson esq., 5 February 1917. From the papers of Jonathan Collinson held by John Higginson of the Fylde Country Life Preservation Society.

29 The National Gas Engine Company to J. Collinson esq., 4 August 1917. From the papers of Jonathan Collinson held by John Higginson of the Fylde Country Life Preservation Society.

30 The National Gas Engine Company to J. Collinson esq., 8 April 1918. From the papers of Jonathan Collinson held by John Higginson of the Fylde Country Life Preservation Society.

31 *The London Gazette*, 14 August 1925, p. 5450.

32 Letter dated 23 September 1925 from J. Collinson to Mr Pelling (solicitor?). From the papers of Jonathan Collinson held by John Higginson of the Fylde Country Life Preservation Society.

33 "Poultry for Profit: Catalogue 1933. Jonathan Collinson, Lingart Poultry Farm, Garstang, Lancs," p. 21. From the papers of Jonathan Collinson held by John Higginson of the Fylde Country Life Preservation Society.

5
WRENNALL'S OF BARTON

Fig 5.1 Jack Wrennall, as drawn by "Furnival" of the *Lancashire Evening Post*.

At a meeting of poultry keepers at the Hoole Village Institute in 1926, Jack Wrennall claimed he had 25 years' experience of the poultry industry,[1] so if this claim is true he developed an interest in poultry around the beginning of the twentieth century. *The Times* reported that his birds were fourth in a laying test in 1910 when he was living at Goff's Cottage, Withnell, Chorley. Second in that same competition was Will Barron, Tom Barron's brother,[2] and shortly after that the two established a working relationship, and Jack Wrennall worked for many years as manager of Will Barron's poultry farm in Bartle.[3] He was still there in 1924 when LUPS gave him the honour of making him president,[4] but about that year he began farming for himself, initially at Lea, and then in 1926 in Barton.[5] He had been an active committee member since the Society's inception, and a frequent speaker at their meetings, particularly in matters relating to breeding. The article announcing his appointment as president refers to Will Barron's farm also as a "poultry appliance works," which suggests that they were making appliances even though they were no longer being advertised so frequently in the local papers.

A Man of Standing

Working for Will Barron gave Mr Wrennall experience of the best utility breeds: Will Barron produced White Leghorns and White Wyandottes, the same breeds his brother specialised in,[6] and they were the breeds Mr Wrennall advocated using.[7] He seems to have been in a position of some status within the company and within the Lancashire poultry fraternity: he frequently gave lectures for LUPS while working for Will Barron, and was a delegate to the National Poultry Parliament, the body which constituted the annual meetings of the National Poultry Council, where he was "Jack Wrennall, Bartle,"[8] with no mention of his being in the employ of Will Barron, and certainly no slightly demeaning appellation which was often used to describe an employee in charge of poultry, "poultryman." In 1924 he was also chairman of the Lancashire Federation of Utility Poultry Societies which united approximately 40 poultry societies throughout the county.[9]

Jack Wrennall involved himself in the community while at Catforth: he worked closely with Tom Barron in setting up the Sports Hall for the village, indeed he "superintended the building, purchased all the material, and charged the club only the actual cost of material and labour."[10] Again at this time, although an employee, he seems to have had a certain amount of standing and autonomy, but he did not use community work to promote himself particularly; after his move to Barton he is rarely heard of in community events.

The Poultry Farm, Barton

Jack Wrennall's poultry farm at Barton, just by the A6, was named assertively "The Poultry Farm, Barton," just as the Barron brothers had named their farms "The Poultry Farm" with the additional name of their own villages. Henry Wrennall, his son, was a partner. From the beginning he manufactured poultry products on his farm, in particular a hover brooder: "Insist on the WRENNALL and accept no other."[11] After retiring as president of LUPS he was still rarely out of the local paper as a judge at agricultural shows across the county and a frequent lecturer, so he maintained a high profile which could only help to market his business. He used his status to increase the membership of LUPS; in October 1927 he was lauded for bringing in 102 new members.[12]

The Wrennall Way

As he began farming for himself relatively late by these poultry farmers' standards, Mr Wrennall's farm did not feature in any poultry journal article, but some of his farming methods can be deduced from his many lectures. The best eggs for incubation came from free-range hens, though he accepted this was not always possible when space was limited.[13] Incubator rooms should be shaded so that the only heat was the relatively controllable artificial heat of the incubator; there should be a constant and reliable source of water for chicks and hens, and he believed in giving the young chicks access to the outside as quickly as possible, in as little as four days and if possible on fresh land to minimise the chance of disease.[14] He believed that brooder floors should be of cinders and cement, and hen cabin floors of wood, with rats kept out by wire netting.[15] When hens were at point of lay and afterwards, cabins should be warm but well ventilated, and those hens were best fed on a mixture of dry and wet mash.[16]

Diversification

Despite his obvious keen interest in poultry, Mr Wrennall, like Mr Collinson, did not, as the irresistible metaphor might have it, put all his eggs in one basket. Besides rearing poultry for eggs, meat and breeding,

Fig. 5.2 The Wrennall trap nest

the Wrennall company also manufactured poultry products such as trap nests, perhaps because of Mr Wrennall's early experience with Will Barron, who also manufactured poultry appliances for a while.

At Barton they moved on to manufacturing poultry housing. "Night arks" were used in the fields to house chicks that no longer needed the brooders, up to point of lay.

Fig. 5.3 Wrennall night arks being loaded at the farm

He also specialised in prefabricated buildings of a standard "24 x 12" size, manufacturing them at his works on the farm and erecting them at the buyer's, and making them easy to dismantle and assemble for movement within the farm or for resale.

The Wrennalls also kept pigs and cows extensively, and in the 1911 census he had been listed as a gardener;[17] he obviously maintained this interest in horticulture and continued market gardening in Barton, especially concentrating on cucumbers and tomatoes, as the advertisement in Figure 5.4 from 1939 shows.[18]

The Farmer and the Hen: A Lancashire Love Story

Fig. 5.4 Wrennall portable cabins

In 1938 there was a brief paragraph on Mr Wrennall in the magazine *Poultry Industry*, praising him for his behind-the-scenes work at the Lancashire laying tests at Hutton, but also for his abilities as a farmer:

> By training he was a gardener, and his interest in gardening is indicated by an acre of tomato houses adjoining his poultry farm and appliance works at Barton. And as if that is not enough to engage his attention, he runs a fine herd of shorthorn cattle and a big herd of Large White pigs. A great man.[19]

Jack Wrennall was killed in a road accident during the blackout on 23 March 1944. His obituary in the local paper praised him as a "shrewd country boy with an inventive turn of mind and any amount of business energy and enterprise," and acknowledged that he "played a prominent part in the politics of the poultry industry."[20] At the time of his death he employed 60 people.[21] The *Preston Guardian* eulogised him in words which echoed those of *Poultry Industry* six years earlier, for "combining with poultry breeding a flourishing business as an appliance maker and tomato grower; he demonstrated to a remarkable degree what is meant by production from a comparatively small area of land and he went from success to success."[22]

Fig. 5.5 Diversification: Jack Wrennall advertisement

Fig. 5.6 Pigs slaughtered on the farm on their way to the butcher

The Farmer and the Hen: A Lancashire Love Story

Fig. 5.7 The Wrennall "office," possibly posed as a joke … but possibly not!

Notes

1   "Chicken Rearing: Hints on Incubator Management," *Preston Guardian*, 6 February 1926, p. 11.
2   "The Utility Poultry Club," *The Times*, 16 February 1910, p. 4.
3   "Chicken Rearing: Hints That Help to Success," *Preston Guardian*, 18 January 1919, p. 8.
4   "Utility Poultry Experts: County Society's New Appointments," *Preston Guardian*, 4 October 1924, p. 3.
5   "Poultry Specialist Killed," *Preston Guardian*, 25 March 1944, p. 5.
6   "Sale of Utility Poultry," *Preston Guardian*, 15 October 1921, p. 5.
7   "Mr Wrennall's Lecture at Longridge," *Preston Guardian*, 5 March 1921, p. 8.
8   "National Poultry Parliament: Meetings at Blackpool," *Preston Guardian*, 30 June 1923, p. 11.
9   "Utility Poultry: County Federation Show at Blackpool," *Preston Guardian*, 6 December 1924, p. 6.
10   "Catforth Sports Club: Opening Ceremony," *Preston Guardian*, 3 February 1923, p. 6.

Wrennall's of Barton

11 "The 'Wrennall' Hover," advertisement in the *Preston Guardian*, 10 March 1923, p. 10. The address is given as "The Poultry Farm and Electric Poultry Appliance, Works, Barton nr. Preston."

12 "Utility Poultry: County Society's Successful Year," *Preston Guardian*, 1 October 1927, p. 10.

13 "Loss of Chicks: Chills the Cause of Heavy Mortality," *Preston Guardian*, 20 February 1926, p. 10.

14 "Chicken Rearing: Expert Describes His Methods," *Preston Guardian*, 15 January 1927, p. 10.

15 "Poultry Ailments: Expert Advice at Preston," *Preston Guardian*, 19 February 1927, p. 5.

16 "Poultry Hints: Mr Wrennall's Lecture at Preston," *Preston Guardian*, 6 October 1923, p. 7.

17 The National Archive UK, 1911 Census, County of Lancaster, Withnell Parish, District 6, p. 4.

18 "Poultry Specialist Killed," p. 5.

19 "Personality Page," *Poultry Industry*, 23 September 1938, p. 559.

20 "Mr J. Wrennall Killed in Road Mishap," *Lancashire Daily Post*, 24 March 1944, p. 4.

21 "Funeral of Mr John Wrennall: Many Tributes," *Preston Guardian*, 1 April 1944, p. 7.

22 "Funeral of Mr John Wrennall," p. 7.

6

BARRON'S OF CATFORTH

Fig. 6.1 Tom Barron in 1913

Tom Barron was born in 1873. His parents were William and Mary Barron, from Rufford in Lancashire, and in 1891 the family was living at Topping House in Catforth, near Preston, and Tom Barron was an apprentice shoemaker.[1] According to Albert Clayton, a local historian related by marriage, his parents were innkeepers who came to Catforth to take charge of The Red Lion, a pub by the Lancaster canal in the village. Initially Mr Barron began keeping a few chickens to supplement his income as a cobbler,[2] but gradually his hobby supplanted his trade. He began commercial breeding at Singleton Farm in 1893.[3] The farm was initially three or seven acres, depending on which source is used, but he gradually expanded it to 75 acres. By 1901 he was married to Harriet, three years his senior.[4] He bought the farm in 1904 from his father, along with three cows and 20 hens, and by 1911 the farm had grown to 23 acres, 10 for the cows and 13 for the home and the hens, and the name had changed to "The Poultry Farm" in Catforth.[5] He was classed as a poultry and dairy farmer in the 1911 census, and had Eric Collinson working for him on the farm, who, though 22, was still described as a "pupil on a poultry farm."[6] Tom and Harriet had two daughters, Olive, who married Frank Leeming in June 1926, and Elsie, who married William Tomlinson in 1931. The Leeming and Tomlinson families actively run the business to this day.

Fig. 6.2 Singleton Farm, 1908: Olive and Elsie Barron. The cabin on the left is the cobbler's shed.

Tom's younger brother William claimed to be living at the same address in 1911, though it is apparent from those census returns near to him that he was actually living about a mile away in Rosemary Lane, Bartle,[7] so whether they were in actual partnership is not clear, but Will too was a poultry farmer. Certainly living memory has their relationship as an occasionally fraught one: allegedly Will Barron had been known to discover when his brother was expecting a delivery at Preston Station and intercept it, keeping it for himself.[8]

A Public Figure

Mr Barron is remembered as a large and quite intimidating figure, though at some time in the 1930s he had a throat operation which caused him to speak in a whisper; however, his voice was no less intimidating for that.[9] He made himself busy in village life. He was a major figure behind raising funds for a village hall as a war memorial,[10] he provided the Girl Guides with a hut and, though belonging to the Church of England himself, helped with the building of a Methodist chapel for the village,[11] and entertained to tea the members of a Catholic pilgrimage to the local Catholic church, St Robert's.[12] When there was a controversy over whether the village hall should have a drinks licence he played a major part in building and arranging events for an alternative and licensed village centre which became known as the Sports Club.[13] The two recreation halls represented something of a schism in the village, even coming into direct rivalry: both institutions organised fancy-dress carnival balls for Easter Monday 1923.[14] He also built several cottages for his workers – indeed it is still a tradition of the company that workers live in Barron's cottages.[15] For 22 years he served on the Preston Rural District Council.[16] Whether conscious or unconscious, there seems to have been something of what Tristram Hunt calls the Victorian "rational and virtuous middle class" about him, when "to be active in the great philanthropic endeavours of the day was essential to rising in public esteem."[17]

The Barron Way

Mr Barron claimed to have become interested in poultry farming because of the columns of Edward Brown in the *Preston Guardian* in the 1890s, but as he was introducing Mr Brown to the LUPS at the time, that may well have been a piece of tactful flattery.[18] He specialised at first in White Wyandottes and White Leghorns, and later expanded and used Rhode Island Reds and Light Sussex. He experimented with cross-breeding, but never more than one cross – two breeds only could make up a strain, never more,[19] though that of course might have been a business tactic to prevent his audiences acquiring their own cockerels and breeding their own chicks from his hens. It is believed that he won his first ever prize in a Northern Utility Society laying trial in 1906 with a pen of White Leghorns. In 1912 he was the first Briton to compete in the North

Fig. 6.3 An inevitable choice of name

American International Laying Competition.[20] An irresistible punning name was not resisted.

International Laying Test Success

In 1919 W. Powell Owen listed the awards Barron's had won up to that date: "42 Silver Cups, 4 Gold Medals, 35 Silver Medals, 52 200 egg ribbons, 11 First Prizes and 11 Second Prizes." These were listed in the firm's catalogue, and Tom Barron told the author, "My catalogue is my silent salesman."[21] The highlight of his achievements in British tests was in 1928–9 when his pen of White Wyandottes broke all records with an average of 262 eggs per bird in 48 weeks.[22] By that time he had branched out even further afield and in 1926 the *Preston Guardian* was recording his success in South African laying trials, and exports of his chicks by air, 2,000 to Moscow and 1,000 to Switzerland.[23] His South African adventure even made the pages of *The Times*.

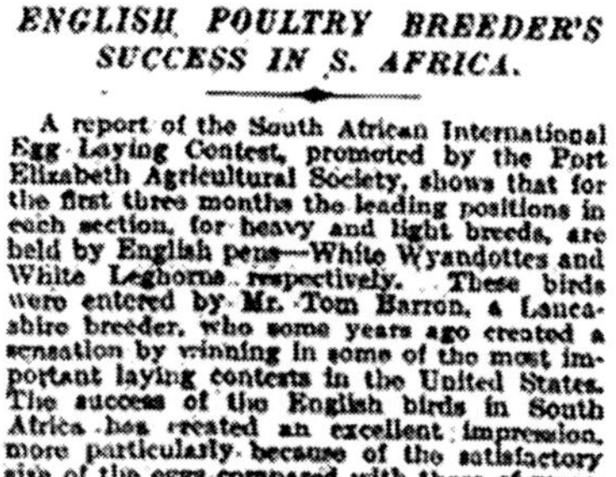

ENGLISH POULTRY BREEDER'S SUCCESS IN S. AFRICA.

A report of the South African International Egg Laying Contest, promoted by the Port Elizabeth Agricultural Society, shows that for the first three months the leading positions in each section, for heavy and light breeds, are held by English pens—White Wyandottes and White Leghorns respectively. These birds were entered by Mr. Tom Barron, a Lancashire breeder, who some years ago created a sensation by winning in some of the most important laying contests in the United States. The success of the English birds in South Africa has created an excellent impression, more particularly because of the satisfactory size of the eggs compared with those of many pens entered by South African and Australian breeders.

Fig. 6.4 Success in South Africa

A Model Farm

Tom Barron's reputation advanced steadily, and within 20 years of his tentative start in farming his farm was featured in a book edited by the editor of *Feathered World*, S. H. Lewer, in 1913, where it was described as "one of the best known farms in the country."[24] In it, Tom Barron explained why he believed that poultry was best kept semi-intensively, and that he had been farming in this way for at least 19 years. His cabins were large enough for 400; diseases, particularly roup, were less prevalent than under the intensive system, and the sliding glass windows near the floor opened easily to let the birds out.

INTERIOR OF SEVENTY-TWO-FOOT LAYING HOUSE

Fig. 6.5 Roomy laying cabin

The grass runs were on either side of the cabin and the birds were allowed out at one side for about a week and then put on to the other side while the first side was allowed to freshen so the land did not become too polluted.[25] The cabin's dimensions were 72 feet long and 18 feet wide.[26]

He was one of the first poultry farmers in the county to use anthracite brooder stoves which could raise 150–200 chicks,[27] and made raising poultry a much better commercial proposition than raising chicks naturally, though he may have been such a public advocate of that particular type to support his brother, Will, who was marketing his own

SEMI-INTENSIVE HOUSE, SEVENTY-TWO FEET LONG, HOUSING 400 LAYERS

Fig. 6.6 Hens in a run at the side of the cabin

"Bartle Standard Anthracite Chicken Brooder" around that time.[28] But it is one example of the readiness to experiment and embrace change which characterises Mr Barron's career, and his information gathering took him far afield: in 1927 he had visited laying tests and Storrs College in Connecticut, and reported his findings to other farmers on his return.[29] His reputation travelled equally as far. An American expert, Dr. Kaupp, on a lecture tour of Britain in 1921 referred to Tom Barron as "one of the world's very best poultry-men who has a very high standing in our country."[30] The American connection continued up to the Second World War: a farming magazine from Iowa proudly advertised personally selected "Tom Barron stock".

His farm was again visited by *Feathered World* editor S. H. Lewer on 11 June 1930. The article which followed is a catalogue of local, national and international laying prizes; unlike Mr Collinson, Mr Barron believed in continuing to test and advertise his stock through competitions. Of interest at this time is the picture of a farm in transition as far as utilities

The Farmer and the Hen: A Lancashire Love Story

Fig. 6.7 Iowa advertisement

are concerned. In one section the chickens were watered by wells and pumps; the next field had Fylde water available so that each cabin had cisterns controlled by ballcocks. The 10,000-egg incubator was about to be replaced with two or more huge electric-powered incubators as the arrival of electricity was imminent; this would represent a saving on space and labour, yet would double the output. Mr Lewer quoted Mr Barron: "I believe in keeping up to date."[31]

The farm also had a meticulous recording scheme housed in a separate office. Hens were identified by rings and toe markings, and records kept of matings and hatchings, and so the pedigree history of any bird could easily be checked. Appropriate bloodlines were identified by use of the trap nest, the selected hens all laying 180 eggs or more per year, and hens were always mated with unrelated cocks.[32] A second, unrelated family was then established, the best layers identified, and then unrelated matings were made between the two lines.[33] The hens for breeding were kept semi-intensively, though the pens could be opened up easily and the hens allowed free range. Mr Barron's own laying stock was by this time kept at Catforth Hall Farm, a separate establishment, and entirely free range at only about 100 birds per acre, the hens sharing the grazing with dairy cows. This suggests that the main aim of the company was to produce day-old chicks or point-of-lay pullets for customers, rather than eggs for consumption, and also that, like those of Mr Collinson and Mr Wrennall, Tom Barron's establishment was not dependent on one product only.[34]

Selling Poultry

Tom Barron was keen to promote poultry farming as an industry, which may, of course, have had the effect of furthering his own business interests, but he extolled its virtues in regions far from his own which suggests self-interest was not a predominant motive. He took part in another Omelette Express, the "Great Eastern Railway Egg Train," the brainchild of the chairman of the Great Eastern Railway Company, Lord Claud Hamilton, which toured East Anglia promoting poultry keeping. He must have been quite an entertainer, too: according to the recollections of a writer in *Poultry Industry* who was on the trip:

> Mr Barron gave a lecture every day ... apart from his magnetic personality he interested many people by using a smart White Leghorn cockerel for demonstration purposes. The bird stood on a table by his side during the lecture, and if it thought he was not

getting enough attention he would peck Mr Barron's sleeve and sometimes crow. Tom Barron and his cockerel made a star turn ... [35]

Man and Myth

Some of the anecdotes about Mr Barron suggest an almost mythological status. At Storrs Agricultural College in the United States he was set the challenge of identifying the one hen in an egg-laying test which hadn't laid a single egg. He succeeded, and later explained that frequent layers lost colour in the leg, so he picked the hen with the brightest yellow legs. So popular were his lectures there that hundreds camped out around the town to hear him.[36] He himself claimed he had sailed on the *Lusitania* the voyage before she was torpedoed,[37] and he was one of those people known instantly by his initials: the *Poultry Industry* writers throughout refer to him as "T.B." as often as "Tom Barron." But as well as the more colourful tales, there is ample evidence of his personality being used as a force for the good of the industry and the farmers themselves. He served on several committees and was a major figure behind the foundation of the LUPS, and through his work with LUPS he showed he was concerned to protect the industry as a whole, and not just to protect his own interests. Many instances have already been given, but he was also a man of instinctive charity. In 1927 floods destroyed several smaller poultry farms in the St Michaels–Churchtown area: ex-servicemen who had taken up the industry after the First World War had been particularly affected, and Tom Barron was anxious that the members of LUPS should help them financially, and contributed personally.[38]

Delegation

His committee commitments must have taken him away from his business for long periods of time, but he seems to have had a knack of employing able managers from all parts of the country. Two of them, Fielding Smith, and a Cornishman, George Wickett, eventually went into partnership together and ran a successful poultry farm in Sussex,[39] and a Scotsman, Tom Elliott, was later appointed manager of the National Laying test at Milford.[40]

Fig. 6.8 Tom Barron

Tom Barron died in 1955, and once again he made the quality newspapers, perhaps appropriately, just below news of a fowl pest outbreak. The report of his death in his local paper was unsurprisingly fuller and more fulsome in its praise; from the opening sentence he was lauded as "the pioneer of commercial poultry-keeping in Lancashire, a man whose name was famous in poultry circles throughout the world." If there is one man behind the creation of the poultry industry in mid-Lancashire who rises above the others, then it is he.

In . Brief

Rochdale Town Council is asking the public to suggest streets which could suitably be used as children's play streets.

John Turnbull, aged 10, of Morton Street, Longsight, Manchester, was knocked down and killed by a lorry in Longsight yesterday.

Mr Paul H. Pearson, the United States Consul in Manchester, is leaving to take up a post in Sweden. His successor, Mr Rufus H. Lane, jun., arrives next month.

Nine further outbreaks of fowl pest have been confirmed in the Longton and Hoole districts, near Preston. Some 15,000 birds have been lost in the past eight days.

Labour retained its seat in the St Paul's ward, Sale, by-election yesterday, when Thomas Arthur Winnington polled 802 votes against 648 by Edward Morgan (C).

Mr Tom Barron, who died at his home at Catforth, near Preston, yesterday, aged 82, was the first chairman of the old National Poultry Council and for 22 years a member of the Preston rural district council.

The Post Office Music Society has collected £1,245 from Post Office staff for a memorial to Kathleen Ferrier, who began her working life as a telephone operator. The memorial takes the form of three grand pianos for Post Office convalescence and holiday centres.

Middleton police have appealed for

Fig. 6.9 Tom Barron's obituary in the *Manchester Guardian*

Notes

1   The National Archive UK, 1891 Census, County of Lancaster, Woodplumpton Parish, Catforth Quarter (District 16), p. 6.
2   "Pioneer of the Poultry Industry," *Preston Guardian*, 8 October 1955, p. 1.
3   Gwen Marquis, 25 April 2012.
4   The National Archive UK, 1901 Census, Lancashire, Woodplumpton Parish, Catforth Quarter (District 12), p. 8.
5   Tom Barron, *How I Breed the 200 Egg Hen: A Complete Treatise of the Methods Used by Tom Barron, England, in Producing Heavy Layers* (Philadelphia. Tom Barron Publishing Co., 1914), p. 11.
6   The National Archive UK, 1911 Census, Lancashire, Woodplumpton Parish, Catforth Quarter (District 12), Schedule 76.
7   The National Archive UK, 1911 Census, Lancashire, Woodplumpton and Broughton, Bartle Quarter (District 11), Schedule 114.
8   Gwen Marquis, who worked in the Barron's office from 1959 to 1961. Interview, 25 April 2012. As told to her by Keith Leeming, Tom Barron's grandson.
9   Winifred Vane, whose father, Bill Knowles, was cowman for Tom Barron in the 1930s. Interview, 25 April 2012.
10   "War Memorial for Catforth," *Preston Guardian*, 12 April 1919, p. 10.
11   Winifred Vane, 25 April 2012.
12   "Catholic Pilgrimage to Catforth," *Preston Guardian*, 19 May 1923, p. 6.
13   "Broughton District: Catforth Sports Club," *Preston Guardian*, 30 April 1921, p. 10.
14   "Catforth Village Hall" and "Carnival Ball at Catforth," *Preston Guardian*, 7 April 1923, p. 10.
15   Gwen Marquis, 25 April 2012. Gwen lives in the original Singleton's Farm, which the company rents to her. Her father had rented a Barron's farm in 1936; Gwen lived there until her marriage in 1962.
16   "In Brief," *Manchester Guardian*, 11 October 1955, p. 16.
17   Tristram Hunt, *Building Jerusalem: The Rise and Fall of the Victorian City* (London. Phoenix/Orion Books, 2005), pp. 176–7.
18   "Mr Edward Brown on Poultry Husbandry in America," *Preston Guardian*, 26 October 1918, p. 4.
19   Gwen Marquis, notes for a talk given to Woodplumpton local history group, August 2008.

20 Gwen Marquis, August 2008.
21 W. Powell-Owen, *Poultry-Keeping on Money-Making Lines* (London. George Newnes, 1919), p. 214.
22 "Pioneer of the Poultry Industry," p. 1.
23 "White Leghorns Make a New Test Record," *Preston Guardian*, 27 November 1926, p. 6.
24 S. H. Lewer, *Wright's Book of Poultry: Revised and Edited in Accordance with the Latest Poultry Club Standards* (London. Cassell and Co., 1913), p. xvi.
25 Lewer, *Wright's Book of Poultry*, pp. xvii–xix.
26 *The Poultry World Annual 1914* (London. The Poultry Press, 1914), p. 166.
27 "Mr J. Collinson's Lecture at Pilling," *Preston Guardian*, 25 January 1919, p. 10.
28 "Will Barron Says …" Advertisement in the *Preston Guardian*, 22 November 1919, p. 8.
29 "Poultry Topics: Messrs Barron and Green on their Canadian Tour," *Preston Guardian*, 3 December 1927, p. 5.
30 "American Scientist's Visit to Lancashire," *Preston Guardian*, 20 August 1921, p. 2.
31 "A Pioneer in Utility Poultry," *The Feathered World*, 18 July 1930, pp. iv–vi.
32 Tom Barron and J. N. Leigh, *The Daily Mail Poultry Book* (London. Associated Newspapers, 1921), p. 110.
33 Barron and Leigh, *Daily Mail Poultry Book*, p. 111.
34 "A Pioneer in Utility Poultry," p. vi.
35 "Reminiscences," *Poultry Industry*, 19 November 1937, p. 7.
36 "Reminiscences," p. 7.
37 "Personality Page," *Poultry Industry*, 29 July 1938, p. 482.
38 "Utility Poultry: County Society's Successful Year," *Preston Guardian*, 1 October 1927, p. 10.
39 "Personality Page," p. 482.
40 "New National Test Director," *Feathered World*, 14 January 1938, p. 6.

CONCLUSION

So what circumstances combined to make the poultry industry in central Lancashire pre-eminent in Britain? Nationally, in the 1850s, interest in poultry was stimulated by the arrival of new Asiatic and American breeds which were bigger than the indigenous chickens and more prolific layers. Royal patronage and the "Cochin mania" also helped to make a formerly unfashionable 'dunghill' bird fashionable, or at least to raise its status.

There was from the first an element of competition, perhaps following on from the cock-fighting tradition, which led to improvements in the strain of chickens. Initially the shows and exhibitions resulted in agreed standards of what constituted quality in a bird, and then the laying tests made the total value of the product important rather than the appearance.

Economic conditions towards the end of the nineteenth century caused farmers to seek to diversify and examine the possibilities for profit that the humble hen offered. Initially poultry's value was in the flexibility hens offered; they could be run alongside other forms of farming. Then as the hen became an accepted form of husbandry it was less the province of the farmer's wife and "hen money," and became a male pursuit: statistics were gathered about individual birds by trap-nesting, experiments were made with breeding, housing, feeding, disease control. In the words of the old "BT" advertisement, poultry became "an –ology."

Once hens had become more integral to British farming, the Government became more involved, particularly when the Great War had exposed Britain's dependence on imported eggs. County farms, agricultural colleges and departments of agriculture within universities were developed; in 1914 the Ministry of Agriculture became involved, national bodies such as the National Poultry Organisation and the National Egg Mark Scheme were created. By the late 1920s and early 1930s, poultry was the subject of several Ministry of Agriculture and Fisheries reports.

Artificial breeding and rearing meant that chickens could be produced in far greater numbers than if naturally bred, and feed and the environment could be more easily controlled. Breeding chickens then became a specialised branch of the industry and one that the small farmer need not worry about – he could buy replacement stock from the specialist. Greater volume of stock led to experiments with different sorts of farming, from regulating the laying year and artificially extending the hours of daylight in winter, to developing new housing and new appliances.

What factors meant that Lancashire in particular could take advantage of these circumstances? Lancashire's association with hens was marked even from the days of cock fighting, which made fowls a familiar part of the landscape from the first in both town and country. "Cocking" and hunting game were activities of the wealthy and the aristocracy but also the interests or employment of the ordinary people, so fowls were woven into the fabric of life, and competitive events such as the mains and later the poultry shows and societies brought excitement and social contact to a wide and varied section of the population.

Conclusion

As the possibilities of the hen as a source of food through eggs and meat came to be realised, so it found a more honourable place on mid-Lancashire farms. These farms tended to be small and family run, and particularly adept at producing perishables for the nearby urban markets: fruit, vegetables, milk, cheese and eggs, and eggs gradually eased their way up the pecking order (a second inevitable metaphor), especially as accounts were more closely kept. The gradually improving late-Victorian transport infrastructure brought the potential markets of industrial south and east Lancashire even nearer.

Opportunities offered by the Land Settlement Act (1919) were taken up enthusiastically, and unlike the sometimes unadventurous traditionalists these newcomers were prepared to try new ideas. There was plenty of support for them. The *Preston Guardian* produced a regular column for poultry enthusiasts, books with sections for the new farmer were published, and most importantly poultry farmers themselves created networks of societies. Town or village poultry societies were linked to larger societies such as LUPS which in turn were linked to the National Utility Poultry Society or other national bodies such as the Scientific Poultry Breeders Association.

Lancashire was one of the first areas of the country whose farmers realised the value of working together. The societies, particularly LUPS, were important in disseminating advice and ideas, in spreading skills, in solving problems; they played a strong role in creating a social bond between poultry farmers. When farmers spoke together they had a greater chance of being heard than if they spoke separately, and they lobbied MPs and government ministers to get what they wanted. Lancashire farmers were also among the first in the country to realise the value of marketing their eggs correctly; for a long time central Lancashire was one of the few areas where the farmers themselves set the prices rather than market forces, and it also had one of the first farmer-run packing stations. In the

1920s when agricultural reports were discussing marketing eggs more professionally, Lancashire farmers were actually doing it.

The larger farmers with the louder voices could perhaps be accused of pursuing a society's aims for their own personal ambition, but there are many instances of the bigger producers protecting the interests of the small farmer, the pounds looking after the pennies. It may not have been for purely altruistic reasons: many small farmers combined would provide a substantial market for the housing, appliances, feeds or replacement stock that the larger ones could provide, thus providing multiple revenue streams, as modern economists might say, for themselves. But the impression is given that the concern to protect the "ten hen men" was out of a concern for the industry as a whole and not just basic self-interest.

For a society to function so effectively, though, it needs strong people in charge. It may be a forum for the exchange of ideas, but someone needs to get those ideas in the first place, and this is why individual farmers such as the ones that have been discussed lie at the heart of the success of this part of the county. Early pioneers such as Richard Teebay and Thomas Sherdley opened up possibilities, and others pursued and refined them.

Those who followed, like Jonathan Collinson, Jack Wrennall and Tom Barron, were proud to celebrate their achievements, prepared to stand their corner, and they were organised, practical and innovative: they entered and won laying tests at local, national and international levels, they wrote to Parliament, they used their contacts to agitate for what they wanted, they stood up for themselves in business, and Tom Barron in particular travelled the world in search of new ideas. They helped with the county farm at Hutton, they put themselves forward as committee members, judges, speakers, and they helped out with community projects; activities which put them, and in consequence their businesses, in the public eye, and earned them respect and status within their own world of poultry

Conclusion

and also within the broader community. They kept records; they utilised science and technology to improve strains, to combat disease, to design appliances and housing, and to benefit the farm economy. They were hard-headed as far as business was concerned: man hours were costed and the most appropriate method of farming used for the amount of land and number of labourers; they kept exhaustive records of their accounts, their laying strains, the number of eggs laid by individual hens, and they culled ruthlessly. That same hard-headedness led them to improve marketing, to reduce the importance of the middleman, the wholesaler and higgler, and to market their eggs through organisations they themselves ran. The collective success of the Lancashire poultry industry is a testament to the driving force of these individuals.

BIBLIOGRAPHY

Oral Histories

John Higginson, Fylde Country Life Preservation Society

Gwen Marquis, Office staff at Tom Barron's 1959–61. Her mother and father rented a Barron's farm from October 1936.

Winifred Vane, Born in 1929: her father, Bill Knowles, worked as cowman for Tom Barron in the 1930s.

Museums and Collections

Fylde Country Life Museum, Farmer Parr's, Rossall Lane, Fleetwood FY7 8JP

Museum of English Rural Life (MERL)

University of Reading archive

Primary Sources

Board of Agriculture and Fisheries, *Wages and Conditions of Employment in Agriculture, Vol. II: Reports* (London. HMSO, 1919)

The Feathered World

The Illustrated London News

Barron, Tom, *How I Breed the 200 Egg Hen: A Complete Treatise of the Methods Used by Tom Barron, England, in Producing Heavy Layers* (Philadelphia. Tom Barron Publishing Co., 1914)

Burnley Express

Lancashire Evening Post and *Lancashire Daily Post*

Lancashire Utility Poultry Society Yearbooks, 1930–40 (Printer: R. Seed, Preston)

Ministry of Agriculture and Fisheries, *Eggs and Poultry: Report of the Reorganisation Commission for Great Britain* (London. HMSO, 1935)

Ministry of Agriculture and Fisheries, *Report on the Marketing of Poultry in England and Wales* (London. HMSO, 1927)

Ministry of Agriculture and Fisheries, *Report on Egg Marketing in England and Wales* (London. HMSO, 1927)

Poultry Industry

Poultry World

Preston Chronicle and *Preston Guardian*

Royal Commission on Agriculture Reports:

Mr Coleman's Report on Northumberland, Lancashire and Cheshire (1882)

Report by Mr Wilson-Fox on the Garstang District of Lancashire and the Glendale District of Northumberland (1894)

The Poultry World

Wallace's Farmer and Iowa Homestead

Secondary Sources

Atkinson, Herbert, *The Old English Game Fowl: Its History, Description, Management and Feeding* (London. The Fanciers' Gazette, 1891)

Barron, Tom, and Leigh, J. N. *The Daily Mail Poultry Book* (London. Associated Newspapers, 1921)

Bibliography

Baum, L. Frank, *The Book of the Hamburgs: A Brief Treatise upon the Mating, Rearing and Management of the Different Varieties of Hamburgs* (Hartford, Connecticut. H. H. Stoddard, 1886)

Baynes, M. *Intensive Poultry Culture* (London. The Feathered World, 3rd edition, 1916.)

Beale, Stephen, *Profitable Poultry Keeping* (Vancouver. George Routledge, 1893.)

Beesley, George, *A Report of the State of Agriculture in Lancashire, with Observations on the Political Position and General Prospects of the Agricultural Classes* (Preston. Dobson and Son, 1849)

Broomhead, William W., *Poultry Breeding and Management* (London. New Era Publishing Co. [1937])

Brown, E. T., *The Poultry Keeper's Text Book* (London. Ward Lock and Co., 1934)

Brown, Edward, *Poultry Keeping as an Industry for Farmers and Cottagers* (London. The Fanciers' Gazette, 1892)

Brown, Sir Edward, *British Poultry Husbandry: Its Evolution and History* (London: Chapman and Hall's 1930 [Read Books facsimile, August 2010])

Brown, Sir Edward, *Memories at Eventide* (Burnley, Lancashire. John Dixon, 1934)

Coles, Rupert, *Development of the Poultry Industry in England and Wales 1945–1959* (London. Poultry World, 1960)

Flatt, C. A., *Poultry Keeping* (London. Methuen and Co., 1920)

Fleming, Ian, *On Her Majesty's Secret Service* (London: Penguin Classics, 2004)

Fowl Pest Review Panel, *Fowl Pest: Newcastle Disease Epidemic, 1970–71: Report of the Review Panel* (London: HMSO, 1971)

Gilbey, Sir Walter, *Farm Stock of Old* (Liss, Hampshire. Spur Publications, 1976). Originally published as *Farm Stock 100 Years Ago* (1910)

Gilbey, Sir Walter, *Poultry-Keeping on Farms and Small Holdings* (London. Vinton and Co., 1904)

Gilbey, Sir Walter, *Sport in the Olden Time* (London. Vinton and Co., 1912)

Halliwell, Stephen K., *Preston Pubs* (Stroud, Gloucestershire. Amberley Publishing, 2014)

Hams, Fred, *Old Poultry Breeds* (Princes Risborough. Shire, 2004)

Heale, W. H., and Reddaway, G. E., *The Intensive System of Poultry Keeping* (London. Crosby Lockwood and Co., 1930.)

Hearson, Chas. & Co., *The Problem Solved: A Practical Treatise on Artificial Incubation and Chicken Rearing* (London. Chas. Hearson & Co., 1894)

Hicks, J. Stephen, *The Possibilities of Modern Poultry Keeping* (London. The Cable Printing and Publishing Company, 1909)

Howkins, Alan, *The Death of Rural England: A Social History of the Countryside since 1900* (London and New York: Routledge, 2004)

Howkins, Alan, *Reshaping Rural England: A Social History 1850–1925* (London and New York. Routledge, 1992)

Hunt, Tristram, *Building Jerusalem: The Rise and Fall of the Victorian City* (London. Phoenix/Orion Books, 2005)

Laslett, Peter, *The World We Have Lost: Further Explored* (London. Routledge, 4th edition, 2004)

Lawler, Andrew, *Why Did the Chicken Cross the World?* (London. Duckworth Overlook, 2015)

Lewer, S. H., *Wright's Book of Poultry: Revised and Edited in Accordance with the Latest Poultry Club Standards* (London. Cassell and Co., 1913)

Lewis, William M., *The People's Practical Poultry Book: A Work on the Breeds, Breeding, Rearing and General Management of Poultry* (New York. The American News Company, 1871.)

Long, James, *Poultry for Prizes and Profit* (London. L. Upcott Gill, undated)

Mingay, G. E., *Rural Life in Victorian England* (Stroud, Gloucestershire. Alan Sutton Publishing, 1990)

Bibliography

Mudie Draper, Rev. H. (ed.), *Scientific Breeders' Association Ltd: Twenty-Second Annual Register* (Rudgwick, Sussex. SPBA, 1937)

Orwin, Christabel S., and Whetham, Edith H., *History of British Agriculture: 1846–1914* (Newton Abbot. David and Charles, 1971)

Perry, P. J., *British Agriculture 1875–1914* (London. Methuen and Co., 1973)

The Poultry Club, *The Standard of Excellence in Exhibition Poultry* (London. The Poultry Club, published by Groombridge and Sons, 1865)

The Poultry World Annual 1914 (London. The Poultry Press, 1914)

Powell-Owen, W., *Poultry-Keeping on Money-Making Lines* (London. George Newnes, 1919)

Priestley, J. B., *English Journey* (London. William Heinemann, Jubilee edition, 1984)

Saunders, Simon M., *Domestic Poultry: Being a Practical Treatise on the Preferable Breeds of Farm-Yard Poultry* (New York. Orange, Judd and Co., 1877.)

Sketchley, W., *The Cocker* (Burton on Trent. J. Croft, 1814)

Smith, H. Easom, *Modern Poultry Development* (Liss, Hampshire. Spur Publications, 1976)

Sturges, Rev. T. W., *Poultry Culture for Profit* (London. MacDonald and Evans, 1907)

Tegetmeier, W. M., *The Poultry Book* (London. Orr and Co., 1856)

Toovey, T. W., *Commercial Poultry Farming* (London. Crosby, Lockwood and Son, 1922)

Whetham, Edith H., *The Agrarian History of England and Wales, Vol. VIII: 1914–1939* (Cambridge. Cambridge University Press, 1978.)

Whittle, Thomas E., *A Triumph of Science: A 70 Year History of the U.K. Poultry Industry* (self-published [1997], MERL Ref. 4534 WHI)

Wright, Lewis, *The New Book of Poultry* (London. Cassell and Co., 1905)

Wright, Lewis, *The Practical Poultry Keeper: A Complete and Standard Guide to the Management of Poultry* (London and New York. Cassell, Petter and Galpin, 1867)

Wright, Lewis, *The Practical Poultry Keeper: A Complete and Standard Guide to the Management of Poultry* (New York. Orange Judd Co., 1894)

Agricultural History Review (Journal of the British Agricultural History Society)

The International Review of Poultry Science (Cambridge Journals)

Past & Present (The Past & Present Society, Oxford University Press)

Internet Sites

http://www.historic-images.co.uk/wp-content/uploads/2012/02/Map-of-Lancashire-from-1937.jpg

Preston Digital Archive: https://www.flickr.com/photos/rpsmithbarney/

ABOUT THE AUTHOR

John Grimbaldeston taught in schools in Liverpool and Preston for over 30 years but was originally from a farming family. After retiring he completed an MA in History at the University of Central Lancashire, and it is the prize-winning dissertation which forms the basis of this book. He now helps out at the Fylde Country Life Museum at Farmer Parr's in Fleetwood, which was the source of much of the information.

Lightning Source UK Ltd.
Milton Keynes UK
UKOW02f2241240416

272856UK00002B/11/P